23

AMERICAN
WAR LIBRARY

★ The Korean War ★

THE WAR
AT HOME

AMERICAN
WAR LIBRARY

★ The Korean War ★

THE WAR
AT HOME

Titles in the American War Library series include:

The Korean War
Life as a POW
Life of an American Soldier
Strategic Battles
Weapons of War

The American Revolution

The Civil War

The Cold War

The Persian Gulf War

The Vietnam War

The War on Terrorism

World War I

World War II

AMERICAN
WAR LIBRARY
★★★★

★ **The Korean War** ★

THE WAR AT HOME

by John F. Wukovits

LUCENT
BOOKS®

THOMSON
─────★─────
GALE

San Diego • Detroit • New York • San Francisco • Cleveland • New Haven, Conn. • Waterville, Maine • London • Munich

LIBRARY OF CONGRESS CATALOGING-IN-PUBLICATION DATA

Wukovits, John F., 1944–
   The war at home / by John F. Wukovits.
      p. cm. — (American war library. The Korean War)
Summary: Discusses the impact of the Korean conflict on life in the United States, including
the dichotomy between post–World War II optimism and consumerism versus the fear of
communism and nuclear bombs. Includes bibliographical references (p.) and index.
   ISBN 1-59018-262-6 (alk. paper)
   1. United States—History—1945–1953—Juvenile literature. 2. United States—Social
conditions—1945—Juvenile literature. 3. Korean War, 1950–1953—United States—
Juvenile literature. 4. Korean War, 1950–1953—Social aspects—Juvenile literature.
[1. United States—History—1945-1953. 2. United States—Social conditions—1945–
3. Korean War, 1950-1953—United States.] I. Title. II. American war library. Korean War.
   E813.W85 2004
   951.904'21'0973—dc22
                                                                          2003014090

Printed in the United States of America

★ Contents ★

A Nation Forged by War

The United States, like many nations, was forged and defined by war. Despite Benjamin Franklin's opinion that "There never was a good war or a bad peace," the United States owes its very existence to the War of Independence, one to which Franklin wholeheartedly subscribed. The country forged by war in 1776 was tempered and made stronger by the Civil War in the 1860s.

The Texas Revolution, the Mexican-American War, and the Spanish-American War expanded the country's borders and gave it overseas possessions. These wars made the United States a world power, but this status came with a price, as the nation became a key but reluctant player in both World War I and World War II.

Each successive war further defined the country's role on the world stage. Following World War II, U.S. foreign policy redefined itself to focus on the role of defender, not only of the freedom of its own citizens, but also of the freedom of people everywhere. During the Cold War that followed World War II until the collapse of the Soviet Union, defending the world meant fighting communism. This goal, manifested in the Korean and Vietnam conflicts, proved elusive, and soured the American public on its achievability. As the United States emerges as the world's sole superpower, American foreign policy has been guided less by national interest and more by protecting international human rights. But as involvement in Somalia and Kosovo proves, this goal has been equally elusive.

As a result, the country's view of itself changed. Bolstered by victories in World Wars I and II, Americans first relished the role of protector. But, as war followed war in a seemingly endless procession, Americans began to doubt their leaders, their motives, and themselves. The Vietnam War especially caused people to question the validity of sending its young people to die in places where they were not particularly wanted and for people who did not seem especially grateful.

While the most obvious changes brought about by America's wars have been geopolitical in nature, many other aspects of society have been touched. War often does not bring about change directly, but acts instead like the catalyst in a chemical reaction, accelerating changes already in progress.

Some of these changes have been societal. The role of women in the United States had been slowly changing, but World War II put thousands into the work force and into uniform. They might have gone back to being housewives after the war, but equality, once experienced, would not be forgotten.

Likewise, wars have accelerated technological change. The necessity for faster airplanes and more destructive bombs led to the development of jet planes and nuclear energy. Artificial fibers developed for parachutes in the 1940s were used in clothing of the 1950s.

Lucent Books' American War Library covers key wars in the development of the nation. Each war is covered in several volumes, to allow for more detail, context, and to provide volumes on often neglected subjects, such as the kamikazes of World War II or the weapons used in the Civil War. As with all Lucent books, notes, annotated bibliographies, and appendixes such as glossaries give students a launching point for further research. In addition, sidebars and archival photographs enhance the text. Together, each volume in the American War Library will aid students in understanding how America's wars have shaped and changed its politics, economics, and society.

A Different Kind of Home Front

People associate numerous activities as defining the home front during America's wars: government bond drives to raise money to finance the war; a string of Hollywood films promoting the nation's effort and encouraging the people to sacrifice in whatever way possible; rationing of important goods such as gasoline, sugar, and meat; popular songs that herald the nation's military; and warm welcomes for returning veterans.

While those images accurately describe conditions back home during World War I and World War II, they bear little similarity with what occurred in the United States during the three years of the Korean War. Instead of rallying behind the troops, digging in for the long haul, and avidly following military operations in faraway Korea, most of the nation's citizens placed the fighting in Korea far down on their list of daily concerns. As long as the war went well for Uncle Sam, people supported the fighting, but once the campaign disintegrated in front of potent enemy assaults, citizens quickly turned away from the tragedy to what they saw as more pleasant pursuits and engaging issues.

This phenomenon produced a completely different home front than the one that existed only five years earlier when the country presented a united front in battling Germany and Japan. Now, getting on with life after the delays and traumas presented by that world war seemed like some overdue award. No one wanted to think of yet another war. Consequently, the home front during the Korean War was not a home front in the more traditional sense, one that organized its total effort behind supporting the troops in the field. The Korean War did not dominate people's attention; it intruded into their lives and prevented them from attaining what they saw as the American dream—family, home, happiness, comfort, and success.

Instead of the war occupying center stage back home, the war and the public's reaction to it formed one piece of a general pattern that enveloped the nation from the end of World War II through the decade of the 1950s. The Korean War home front, or the lack of one, helped produce a host of unique trends that marked the decade.

An Inaccurate Image

The popular image of the 1950s that comes from television shows like *Happy Days* and movies such as *Back to the Future* is one of simplicity and stability. Adults lent calmness and order to families, and sons and daughters engaged in clean, wholesome fun. But this image is only partially accurate. Although people who lived in the United States during the Korean War longed for peace and serenity, and sometimes achieved it, they were caught up in a turbulent time that was fraught with fear and threats, disruptions to society, alienation, turmoil, and tribulation. Often the discord in society was made more prominent because it clashed with the prosperity evident in the post–World War II years.

A family in Long Island, New York, hides inside their personal underground bomb shelter, stocked with food and first-aid rations.

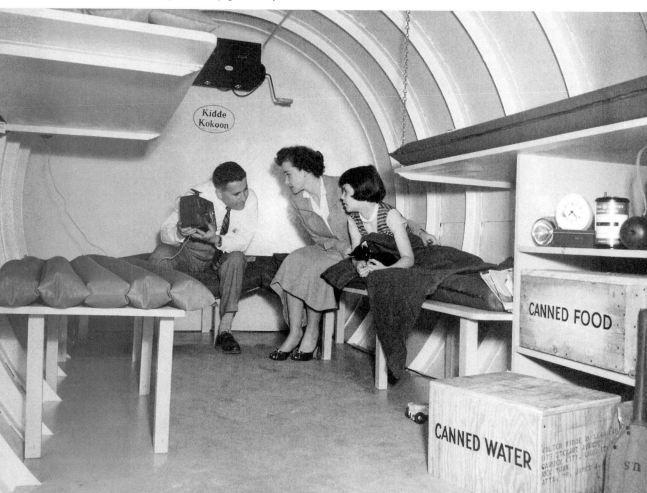

This produced a surreal world in which Americans purchased new cars and home appliances while at the same time constructed bomb shelters in their backyards. It was almost as if the home front during and immediately after the Korean War suffered from a split personality.

This division started when military veterans streamed home following World War II. After ten years of suffering through the Great Depression and four years battling the Nazi war machine in Europe and the Japanese in the Pacific, Americans could finally focus on things besides sacrifice, bloodshed, and destruction. People longed to marry, raise families, start careers, and purchase their own homes. Men and women in and out of the military had given up so much to attain victory, had placed families and jobs on hold for so long, that now a strong desire to possess things swept the nation. Finally, people could look ahead with optimism that their promised land lay immediately before their eyes.

Fear and Paranoia

The ideal, however, did not match the reality. Although consumers flocked to stores in record numbers to purchase television sets and furniture to place in their new homes and new automobiles to drive to their jobs, a series of events kept them from truly enjoying the newfound sense of prosperity. The most frightening specter appeared in the form of international communism, the dictatorial system of government existing in the Soviet Union that appeared ready to sweep into other nations, including the United States. Communism threatened to disrupt world peace, or at least the version of world peace envisioned by Western democracies. This friction between Western democracies, headed by the United States, and Communist nations, with ties to the Soviet Union, was labeled the Cold War. The two superpowers' jockeying for influence in the world involved little actual confrontation but much intrigue and political wrangling. Cold War competition grabbed headlines from 1945 until well beyond the 1950s. The Korean War, from 1950 through 1953, grabbed a large portion of those headlines because it was one event in which the Cold War turned hot.

For a time Americans relaxed in the knowledge that their nation possessed the only atom bombs in the world, but that sense of security ended in 1949 when the Soviet Union perfected its own atomic weapon. Now, rather than enjoying sole superpower status, the United States suddenly faced a potent challenger. Communism no longer seemed to be a distant and inferior threat; the Soviet Union could deliver mass destruction to the American continent if provoked.

Fear and paranoia swept the nation. Were Communists already inside the United States working as spies and saboteurs to destroy the country's foundations? No longer militarily safe behind its protective shores, America now also felt threatened from within. Perhaps the Soviets did not want to destroy America militarily as much as they wanted to subvert the country's democratic principles.

Those fears multiplied in 1950 when President Harry S. Truman committed U.S. military forces to the fighting in distant Korea, a land few Americans knew much about, to prevent Communist North Korea from overrunning South Korea. Americans at first supported the government's actions, for here at least was an attempt to check the spread of communism (which had already swallowed up much of Eastern Europe). But when the fighting in the Southeast Asian nation quickly turned against the United States, people on the home front—weary from the casualty list of World War II—started to have doubts. Support for President Truman plunged, especially after he fired the nation's most renowned military officer, General Douglas MacArthur, for criticizing the government's lack of resolve in ridding the Korean peninsula of Communists.

Unlike the previous war, when Americans saved scraps of steel and rubber for the war effort and sang patriotic songs, no similar sense of fervor existed. Americans wondered why this small Asian nation was so difficult to subdue. As the war raged on without an appropriate answer, the public's impatience rose to high pitch. Instead of a speedy victory, American soldiers became embroiled in a stalemate that lasted until war's end in 1953. The American public, accustomed to the momentum and progress that typified U.S. operations in World War II, stood on the sidelines in 1950 and 1951 and watched

as fighting raged with no end in sight. People wanted the war to be resolved as quickly as possible so they could finally get on with lives that had already been placed on hold by the depression and World War II.

The Quest for Normalcy

War's end would not solve Americans' dilemma, however, for communism lurked beyond the battlefield. During the early 1950s, while U.S. soldiers and sailors battled on the frigid hills of Korea and on the waters offshore, American citizens back home contended with real and supposed Communist subterfuge from within. Senator Joseph McCarthy sparked a national drive to uncover spies, and everything from Hollywood films to comic books warned the nation of the new peril posed by agents of a foreign government working to undermine democracy in the United States. Americans not only faced perils on the battlefields of Korea but also stared at an equally dangerous situation within their own borders. The sense of security delivered by victory in World War II and sustained by the atomic monopoly had now given way to a double-edged paranoia—would communism rush to victory overseas while also boring into every aspect of American society?

This double threat sparked an even stronger desire among Americans to find serenity in their lives. People married younger, started families sooner, and abandoned the hustle and bustle of larger cities to live in one of the new suburbs that rose in the peaceful countryside. New industries

The Iron Curtain

British statesman Winston Churchill coined a phrase that captured the tension of the early 1950s in a March 1946 speech delivered at tiny Westminster College in Fulton, Missouri. When asked by President Harry Truman if he would agree to address the college, Churchill eagerly accepted, stating that he had a few things on his mind that needed airing.

People in the audience had no inkling that they were about to listen to a master orator deliver yet another of his famous lines. The man who stirred his nation to victory in World War II, in part because of his moving utterances, again produced words that reverberated throughout the world.

In his book *The Crucial Decade—and After: America, 1945–1960,* historian Eric F. Goldman includes Churchill's words. Churchill warned that tyranny, in the form of international communism, threatened world peace and proclaimed in now-famous words that in Europe, "from Stettin in the Baltic to Trieste in the Adriatic an iron curtain has descended across the Continent." Churchill added that the democratic nations had to unite against the Soviet Union, for he was "convinced that there is nothing they admire so much as strength, and there is nothing for which they have less respect than for weakness, especially military weakness."

Churchill's description of an iron curtain across Europe remained in popular usage for the next forty years. Only with the downfall of the Soviet Union did people no longer need to view Europe as two separate entities.

Headlines from September 1949 announce the Soviet Union's successful atomic bomb test.

materialized that catered to their needs. Appliance stores, fast-food restaurants, and motel chains provided for consumers who wanted their needs attended to quickly. Detroit's automotive industry encouraged a national longing to have bigger, better, and faster cars by introducing new models every year.

It was almost as if the country believed that if it focused on prosperity, family, and other domestic concerns, communism would, in time, disappear. If Americans could re-create the perfect home and family, and persuade others to conform to the norm, they could ignore other ills that plagued the nation.

"The average American male stands five feet nine inches tall, weighs 158 pounds, prefers brunettes, baseball, beefsteak and French fried potatoes, and thinks the ability

Harry S. Truman

The thirty-third president of the United States was born on May 8, 1884, in Lamar, Missouri. During World War I he enlisted in the artillery, where he served with distinction in France as captain of an artillery unit.

He returned from the war to open a clothing store in Missouri, but he entered politics when the firm went bankrupt. As a Democrat, Truman served as county judge from 1922 to 1934, at which time he won election as U.S. senator from Missouri.

Truman ascended to the highest ranks of government in 1944 when President Franklin D. Roosevelt named him as his vice presidential candidate for that year's fall elections, which the duo won. The following spring, Truman suddenly found himself as the leader of the country when Roosevelt died on April 12.

Truman showed an ability to lead. He continued to implement Roosevelt's policies while gathering around him a circle of advisers upon whom he could place his trust. He needed it, for Truman had to deal with the titanic world figures of the day, especially the Soviet Union's Joseph Stalin and Great Britain's Winston Churchill. To hasten the war's end, Truman approved use of the first atom bomb, which was subsequently dropped on Hiroshima on August 6, 1945. The Japanese government, after realizing it could hold out no longer in light of the frightening atomic weapon, surrendered in September.

Truman never shied from making the tough decision, as his choice to use the world's initial atom bomb shows. To remind himself that final responsibility rested with him, Truman kept on his desk a sign that read, "The Buck Stops Here!"

After winning election in 1948 and leading the nation during much of the Korean War, Truman declined to run again in 1952. He retired to Missouri, where he wrote his memoirs. Truman died on December 26, 1972, and was buried in the courtyard of the Truman Library.

to run a home smoothly and efficiently is the most important quality in a wife,"[1] stated an article in a 1954 *Reader's Digest*. Such an assessment reveals a belief that the current unsettling trends could be checked by rigidly maintaining a comfortable norm that focused on domestic tranquility.

Departures from the Norm

Unfortunately, the home front during the Korean War failed to offer the stability that many Americans coveted. Instead, more shocks, especially in the area of civil rights, rattled the country's foundations. African Americans, weary of segregation's bitter legacy and tired of dying on battlefields for a nation that would not grant them full equality, adopted a more confrontational manner in the first half of the decade. This sparked actions that directly resulted in the famed civil rights movement that battled for greater freedoms for African Americans throughout the fifties and sixties.

Seeking rights that most Americans took for granted, a Topeka, Kansas, resident forced the local school system to abandon segregated schools. The horrible murder of a teenage African American named Emmett Till produced an outrage that fueled further unrest. Shortly after, Rosa Parks refused to abandon her seat on a Montgomery, Alabama, bus and move to the all-black section in the rear. A citywide boycott of the busing system by Montgomery's African American population followed Parks's arrest, which in turn drew the attention of a young Atlanta, Georgia, minister named Martin Luther King Jr. The civil rights movement gained full stride once these events fell into place, all in part spurred by developments that occurred during the Korean War.

Civil rights was not the only turbulent arena in the United States during the Korean War. An upswing in the incidents of juvenile delinquency caused parents to wonder what had happened to decency and morals and to worry about the lack of stability in the family unit. Strange music, strange clothing, and more liberal youth culture placed incredible strains on older

Rosa Parks is fingerprinted after being arrested for refusing to move to the black section of a Montgomery, Alabama, bus.

Americans who yearned for calm instead of rebelliousness.

"The Pattern of Civilization"

The entertainment world mirrored the hectic current events unfolding in the nation. As if reflecting parental desire for normalcy, television shows such as *The Adventures of Ozzie and Harriet* presented ideal families consisting of two parents and well-adjusted teenage sons and daughters. As was true of so much in the early and mid-1950s, however, the image stood miles from reality. Wholesome families existed everywhere, of course, but so, too, did dysfunctional family units broken from divorce, death, and abandonment and populated by people experiencing an array of emotions from delight to misery.

Entertainment added its own assault on the family. Beatniks, a group of poets and novelists who assembled in New York and San Francisco, assailed current society as being hypocritical and urged readers to abandon traditional ways. At the same time, Elvis Presley, Bill Haley, and other performers so altered the musical landscape that a new term was coined to label their frenetic sounds—*rock and roll*. And in film, actors such as Marlon Brando and James Dean

Bill Haley and His Comets were one of the pioneers of rock-and-roll music.

built movie careers playing the youthful, misunderstood rebel.

Consequently, rather than being a time of national unity as seemingly characterized the home front during World War II, the home front in the Korean War offered a unique mixture of patriotism, paranoia, economic abundance, impatience with the war effort, and fear of annihilation from ever-growing arsenals of nuclear weapons. And while the nation suffered from this schizophrenia, the democracies of the world looked to the United States to take a strong stand against communism and lead by example.

"We are living in one of the great watershed periods of history," proclaimed the 1952 Democratic presidential candidate Adlai Stevenson. He added that the era "may well fix the pattern of civilization for many generations to come. God has set for us an awesome mission: nothing less than the leadership of the free world."[2] But even Stevenson was unaware of whether Americans would embrace that mission or ask the cost of assuming such a responsibility.

The clash between the desire for a routine life and the unpleasantness of free-world leadership, including the fight for Korea, produced a chaotic epoch in American history that led to drastic change in many fields, including politics, society, the family, entertainment, and science. This, more than combat from a distant land, occupied the nation during the early 1950s.

"Now a Different World"

T he feeling of unease that citizens in the United States felt during the 1950s had its roots in World War II. The United States and the Soviet Union, former allies who had joined forces to defeat Adolf Hitler's Nazi Germany, now stood at opposite ends of the political spectrum. The democratic United States touted one way of life, and the Communist-controlled Soviet Union boasted that its way of governing—supposedly based on a classless social order—stood as the wave of the future. Soviet leader Joseph Stalin even stated that communism and capitalism, the society prevailing in democracies, were so incompatible that a war was inevitable.

Americans only had to look to Eastern Europe to see the disturbing trend. The Soviet Union had already implanted its system in those nations that it overran during the war, and the Russians stood poised to expand their influence elsewhere in Europe. Communist governments, all under the iron control of Moscow, appeared in Albania, Bulgaria, Czechoslovakia, Hungary, Romania, and Poland. Americans wondered how far throughout the world the Soviet government was willing to go to spread its Communist rule.

The American public, however, felt content that the Soviets could not push their gains any farther without military action. Such an event would undoubtedly trigger a U.S. response, and the Russians lacked one weapon that the U.S. arsenal boasted—atomic bombs. As long as the United States maintained an atomic monopoly, what country would dare to step forward and challenge it? Americans lived and worked with the knowledge that no one in the world could counter America's ultimate bargaining chip, a feeling that imparted a tremendous sense of security as the nation approached 1950. That feeling did not last long, however, as the Soviet Union made great strides toward equalizing the situation, a condition that caused great consternation in the United States.

The Soviet Union Catches Up

U.S. scientists stated that the country would enjoy this military advantage at least until the mid-1950s, when they believed Soviet scientists would finally perfect a nuclear weapon. That prediction, and the sense of security that prevailed in the United States, quickly dissolved on September 3, 1949, when long-range reconnaissance aircraft recorded unusually high levels of radioactivity in the atmosphere, indicating a likely Soviet atom bomb test. When further flights

A giant mushroom cloud rises from the waters of Bikini lagoon during a U.S. atomic bomb test in 1946.

picked up even stronger levels of radioactivity, scientists reported to President Harry S. Truman that the Soviet Union had joined the United States in possessing an atom bomb. The stunned president repeatedly asked his scientific advisers if their information was correct. When he informed top political leaders of the shocking development, Republican senator Arthur Vandenberg exclaimed that this "is now a different world."[3]

Truman and the rest of the nation faced the numbing realization that they could no longer hide beneath an atomic umbrella. The principal U.S. rival in the postwar world now possessed the bomb, and boasted the conventional military strength to support it. Instead of enjoying a secure feeling of peace, Americans entered an era when fear of "the bomb" set the tone. Ideological conflict with the Soviet Union could lead to military confrontation, and that certainly could result in nuclear armageddon. The possibility of widespread death and destruction gripped a nation not used to facing that specter. Fear and uneasiness hovered across America.

The Hydrogen Bomb

Truman took quick action to allay public fears. On January 31, 1950, he vowed to protect the country from foreign aggression—in this case, the Soviet Union—and ordered scientists to move ahead in the testing of a weapon that both thrilled and terrorized scientists for the frightening potential of its destructiveness—the hydrogen bomb. Far

more potent than the atom bombs that devastated Hiroshima and Nagasaki to end the war with Japan, the hydrogen bomb supposedly could unleash 1 million tons of TNT, one-third the amount of all the firepower used during World War II. Truman wondered whether he should permit the testing of such a cataclysmic bomb, but when advisers assured him that the Soviet Union would undoubtedly rush ahead with its own tests, he concluded he had little choice.

A race now commenced between the United States and the Soviet Union to see which nation could perfect the first hydrogen bomb and thereby maintain nuclear dominance, a race that took on a heightened sense of urgency when war broke out on the Korean peninsula. As American ground, air, and naval forces battled Communist opponents in Korea, noted scientist Edward Teller directed a massive effort that culminated on November 1, 1952, with the initial testing of a hydrogen bomb. Results proved both satisfying and disturbing, for the bomb produced a force more than one thousand times greater than the bomb that had turned Hiroshima to ashes.

One of the witnesses to the test, which occurred over a small island in the Pacific Ocean, later wrote of the bomb's power:

The fireball expanded to three miles in diameter. Observers, all evacuated to 40 miles or more away, saw millions of gallons of lagoon water turned to steam, appear as a giant bubble. When the steam

had evaporated, they saw that the island of Elugelab where the bomb had been, had vanished, vaporized also. In its place a crater one half mile deep and two miles wide had been born in the reef. [4]

The United States could not rest on its achievement, however, as the Soviet Union doggedly pursued its own nuclear program. To maintain an edge, American scientists and military planners had to keep one step ahead of their Communist counterparts, in-

Smoke and radioactivity from the first hydrogen bomb test billows across one hundred miles of sky.

cluding the development of a fleet of long-range bombers to deliver the atom and hydrogen bombs. By the mid-1950s American factories produced bombers that reached speeds of six hundred miles per hour and flew at altitudes of forty-five thousand feet. Under the leadership of the cigar-chewing, profanity-spewing General Curtis LeMay, a

"A Burning, Searing Death"

Fear of the danger posed by the arms race was evident in all sections of society. Especially potent was the anguish suffered by the nation's youth, who had so much to look forward to in life yet wondered if they would live to realize any of it. The February 1950 issue of *Life* magazine quoted from an essay written by a fourteen-year-old schoolboy from Los Angeles. His teacher had asked the class to write about the nation's decision to build a hydrogen bomb. The words are included in Paul Boyer's *By the Bomb's Early Light.*

The hydrogen bomb reeks with death. Death, death to thousands. A burning, searing death, a death that is horrible, lasting death. The most horrible death man has invented; the destroying annihilating death of atomic energy. The poisoning, killing, destroying death. Death of the ages, of man, the lasting death.

military man who favored attacking the Soviet military machine before it became too strong, the number of bombers in the American arsenal quadrupled from 1949 to 1955.

Nuclear tests followed, one after the other, until they almost became a staple of American life. Newspapers and magazines printed the results with regularity and marked the spiraling increase in destructiveness with each new variant of the bomb. For some, the news posed little threat at all. One California family that lived near a testing ground became so accustomed to seeing bright flashes and feeling their home shake from the impacts that they hardly thought of the tests. One night a noise awakened them. "What's that?" asked the father, with evident concern in his voice. "Oh, go back to sleep," said his wife. "It's only the atomic bomb." The man settled back, confident that all was well. "All right. I was afraid one of the kids had fallen out of bed."[5]

For others, the arms race appeared to be spinning so madly out of control that the threat of universal destruction, the genera-tion's Grim Reaper, stared them in the face. First of all, whenever the United States developed a more powerful bomb, it seemed the Soviet Union followed closely behind with its own version. Once the Communist nation completed testing on its own hydrogen bomb on November 22, 1955, the United States had the option of either building stronger bombs, more bombs, or allowing its opponent to surpass it in nuclear strength. The government could hardly allow the final alternative to occur.

"General Annihilation Beckons"

People warned about the dangers of slipping into an arms race from which no nation could escape. One writer in 1950 stated that the desire to possess a nuclear arsenal "promises only to bring the nightmares, the hallucinations, the convulsions of a final global dementia."[6]

The *Saturday Evening Post*, one of the most respected magazines of its day, proclaimed that the use of such frightful weapons could have complications that no one foresees. "We fear terribly that what we do in a new war will be as wrong and stupid as much of what we did in the last one, but like a man in a dream, we see no way to reverse the field."[7]

Albert Einstein, the esteemed scientist whose groundbreaking work helped lay the foundation for development of the atom bomb, warned of radioactive poisoning of the atmosphere from numerous bomb tests and "hence annihilation of any life on earth has been brought within the range of technical possibilities. General annihilation beckons."[8]

Radioactive fallout from testing became another national concern. For instance, radioactive ash from a series of tests blanketed seven thousand square miles of the Pacific Ocean. The ash posed such a hazard that a group of Japanese fisherman working eighty miles from the blast perished, and the U.S. government evacuated islanders in the region. Radioactive rain fell on Chicago, Illinois. Physicians, including the noted discoverer of a cure for polio, Jonas Salk,

Albert Einstein warns of the threat of radioactive poisoning caused by bomb tests.

warned that fallout could cause leukemia, bone cancer, and genetic alterations.

Duck and Cover

The government and individual citizens tried to implement measures to safeguard the population from possible atomic war. In the early 1950s pamphlets urged citizens to be prepared for such emergencies. One such pamphlet asserted, "A population that has *planned* to survive will survive."[9] The government advised people to purchase Geiger counters, devices that measured the amount of radiation in the air, and suggested that glass in homes and businesses be replaced with less breakable plexiglas. Teachers instructed students that, should an atomic bomb explode during school, they were to crawl under their desks, huddle over, and face the floor. Bert the Turtle, a cartoon animal created by the government during those years, urged children to "duck and cover" whenever near a nuclear blast.

In more than one suburb, homeowners dug fallout shelters, complete with water and canned food, in their backyards. Some even debated the morality of refusing a spot in the cramped quarters to a shelterless neighbor. Many claimed that the right of self-defense, guaranteed by the Constitution, enabled citizens to keep out, even by shooting, unwelcome intruders. One Catholic priest justified the action by stating that self-defense was a traditional Christian belief.

The government divided the nation into sectors for civil defense, then issued infor-

mation on what people should do in an emergency. One practice test sent ten thousand Washington, D.C., government workers rushing from their offices to secret centers while a helicopter whisked President Dwight D. Eisenhower to an underground command post in Maryland.

The nuclear race grew to such proportions that both superpowers possessed the means with which to destroy the world. That sobering thought frightened many people on the home front during the Korean War and immediately after, but many saw no way out of the tangle. President Eisenhower, Truman's successor, spoke of the absurdity of incinerating the planet upon which everyone lived and stated the world had reached the point "where there is just no alternative to peace."[10]

People were reminded of the famous yet frightful utterance of Albert Einstein when a group of reporters asked him what weapons would be used in World War III. He replied that he had no idea, but that he could tell them the main weapons of World War IV. When a reporter asked him to elaborate, Einstein answered that it would be fought with sticks and stones.

The Truman Doctrine

Other world events in the years before, during, and immediately after the Korean War contributed to the general feeling of insecurity on the home front. The spread of communism outside the Soviet Union to other countries prodded President Truman into announcing on March 12, 1947, the

U.S. president Harry S. Truman (second from left) greets General Dwight D. Eisenhower.

Truman Doctrine. This basic statement formed the bedrock of post–World War II policy and committed the United States to containing the spread of communism. "We must assist free people to work out their own destinies in their own way," promised Truman, who added that the country would also support those nations who "are resisting attempted subjugation by armed minorities or by outside pressures."[11] For instance, between 1947 and 1950 the United States committed more than $400 million in assistance to democratic governments in Greece and Turkey that were threatened by Communist subversion.

Truman's declaration and Joseph Stalin's actions led to what has been labeled as the Cold War—a condition of animosity between the two countries that fell short of open military confrontation. The superpowers contested for control and influence

Television and the Communists

Television offered a few other selections dealing with the war against communism besides *I Led Three Lives.* Most series failed to last longer than one season. *Biff Baker, U.S.A.* starred Alan Hale Jr. as a traveling American spy posing as a businessman dealing in the import-export trade. As he moved in and out of the many countries he visited each week, he collected information for his government or broke up groups of Communist "thugs."

Individual episodes in other series or special programming performed better. A 1952 episode of *Sky King,* a show about a pilot, had Sky King uncovering a group of Chinese secret agents. In 1954 the *Motorola TV Hour* aired "Atomic Attack," a program that followed a New York family dealing with the aftermath of a fictional nuclear attack. The next year the National Broadcasting Corporation presented the historical special *Nightmare in Red,* an account of the rise of communism in Russia.

Most of these programs did little more than briefly entertain or educate the audience. Few viewers remembered them after the decade ended.

in other regions around the world in an immense competition to spread their systems of government.

The Truman administration took other steps. In June, Secretary of State George C. Marshall announced the Marshall Plan, a package of economic and financial aid to Europe. The U.S. government formulated this aid package ostensibly to help Europe rebuild its war-torn countries, but it also served as a method of ensuring that communism did not take advantage of weakened nations. This was the Truman Doctrine in action.

Truman's declaration meant that the United States would act as the democratic world's policeman in the struggle to defeat communism. Wherever strife flared, the United States would rush in aid or military forces to counter it. The lines had been drawn between two opposing worlds; an archenemy had been created for the United States. The statement also meant that the American public, after supporting a unified

effort to defeat Germany and Japan, faced further action against a new enemy at a time when most Americans dreamed of enjoying the fruits of peace.

Tension Mounts

Two other pronouncements established American foreign and domestic policy toward communism in the 1950s. On March 22, 1947, Truman issued Executive Order 9835, which called for a loyalty examination for all government workers to ferret out possible traitors. From its inception until the end of 1952, the government investigated more than 6 million people, resulting in the termination of five hundred people who were found to have questionable loyalty. This presidential order, the first in a series of actions that resulted out of fear of Communist domination, foreshadowed other, more sinister, campaigns to follow.

Additional occurrences proved to people in the United States that communism posed a great and immediate threat. In 1948 the Soviet Union attempted to force the U.S. military out of Berlin—it had been stationed there since the end of World War II, but the Soviet Union retained control of the rest of Germany—by shutting down all road, water, and railway traffic into that German capital. A determined American response, however, in the form of a mass airlift of food and other essential supplies, caused Stalin to lift the blockade the next year.

Sensing heightened tension with the Soviet Union, in April 1949 Truman aligned the nation with Canada, Britain, France, and eight other countries to form the North Atlantic Treaty Organization (NATO). The members stated that an attack against any

President Truman addresses an audience of diplomats during the signing of the North Atlantic Treaty in April 1949.

one of them would be considered an attack on all of them. Leaders in the Soviet Union clearly understood that this warning was aimed at them.

Communists threatened to seize control in China following World War II. After the Japanese had been defeated, civil war broke out between the Nationalists, led by Chiang Kai-shek, and Mao Tse-tung's Chinese Communists. Despite sending $2 billion worth of weapons and supplies to the Nationalists, the Truman government could not prevent the Communists from defeating Chiang Kai-shek. In May 1949, Mao drove his opponent from mainland China.

The successful Communist drive in China raised concerns in Washington and the rest of the nation about the country's ability to contain communism. Stalin tightly held Eastern Europe under his Communist rule, and now China had fallen. What nation would be targeted next?

"Embroilment in a Hopeless Cause"

Only five brief years after the end of World War II—a conflict so devastating that some nations never regained their standing in the world and many individuals could only with difficulty reestablish normal lives—hostilities flared on a rugged section of the Asian continent. Divided into the Communist-controlled North Korea and the democratic South Korea, the country provided one of the harshest battlegrounds possible. Rugged mountains, searing summer heat, and frigid winter cold made for insufferable fighting conditions. It was here, in 1950, that U.S. military forces once again were deployed in combat.

At first, people on the home front lent avid encouragement to the fighting in Korea, just as they had done during World War II. As conditions on the battlefield deteriorated and casualties mounted, however, the support quickly dissipated. Americans had had enough of bloodshed and sacrifice in fighting what they saw as major threats from Hitler's Germany and the legions in Japan.

They had little use for a war in a locale few knew about before 1950. As long as the fighting was quick and the United States was triumphant, people went along with it. Events in Korea did not fit that script, however.

"Time to Draw a Line"

President Truman viewed with alarm the situation in Korea when, on June 25, 1950, Communist units from North Korea poured across the 38th parallel into South Korea, intent on toppling the government and uniting all of Korea under the Communist regime. As conditions turned critical for South Korea, whose forces rapidly retreated before the better-equipped and better-trained Communist soldiers, Truman decided that the United States had to intervene to prevent communism from spreading into another land.

When Truman announced on June 27 that he had issued orders sending American soldiers into the Korean conflict, public

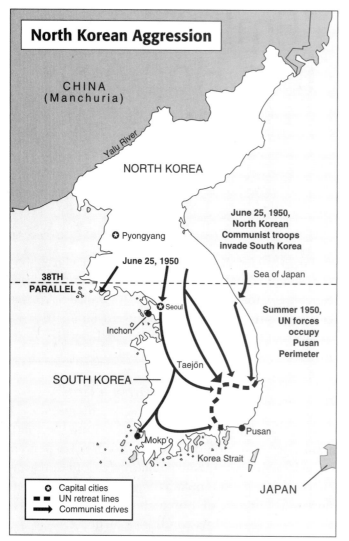

North Korean Aggression

CHINA
(Manchuria)

Yalu River

NORTH KOREA

⊗ Pyongyang

June 25, 1950

38TH
PARALLEL

⊗ Seoul

Inchon

Taejŏn

SOUTH KOREA

Mokp'o

Korea Strait

June 25, 1950,
North Korean
Communist troops
invade South Korea

Sea of Japan

Summer 1950,
UN forces
occupy
Pusan
Perimeter

● Pusan

JAPAN

⊗ Capital cities
■ ■ UN retreat lines
➤ Communist drives

entire world. If communism had to be stopped, better to do it early and in a foreign land rather than inside America's borders.

The press also praised the president's action. A Republican newspaper, the *New York Herald-Tribune,* stated on June 27 of the Democrat Truman, "The President has acted—and spoken—with a magnificent courage and terse decision. . . . It was time to draw a line—somewhere, somehow." [12]

Three days later the *New York Times* offered a headline proclaiming "Democracy Takes Its Stand." [13] Even the *Chicago Tribune,* long a harsh critic of Democrat leaders, agreed that Truman basked in enormous popularity.

Other democratic governments offered their support as well. A French official praised Truman for issuing a firm commitment to halt communism, and the British ambassador to the United States, Oliver Franks, notified his superiors in London that Truman enjoyed newfound popularity at home and overseas. "The average American is pleased that the United States has for once boldly taken the initiative, proud that it has called the Soviet bluff and 'won't let them get away with it.' Virtually all shades of opinion wholeheartedly support the President." [14]

opinion overwhelmingly supported him. Seventy-five percent of the country approved of his actions, and mail piled into the White House with favorable letters outdistancing critical remarks by a ten to one margin. American citizens assumed the actions by North Korea were directed by the Soviet Union as part of its desire to take over the

Truman's approval ratings soared even further on July 8, when he named World War II military hero Douglas MacArthur to command United Nations (UN) forces in Korea. The American public felt secure with MacArthur in charge. After all, he helped orchestrate the defeat of Japan in World War II. The nation headed to war with a confidence born of past military splendors and present military strength.

"The Worst Possible Location"

To the surprise of most every American, the fighting in Korea failed to follow the pattern set in World War II. Instead of American troops wiping out the enemy, well-trained North Koreans swept by opposition units and soon had the Americans and their UN allies on the run. A reporter for the *New York Herald-Tribune*, Marguerite Higgins, wrote of soldiers abandoning their posts in

Douglas MacArthur

General MacArthur and President Truman failed to agree on many issues, but one with which they would both concur was the military genius of General MacArthur. His family's lineage in the U.S. services almost guaranteed that he, too, would exhibit leadership talent.

Born in 1880 to Arthur MacArthur, who won the Medal of Honor during the Civil War, Douglas MacArthur graduated from the West Point military academy in 1903. Service in World War I, where he commanded a brigade of troops and was wounded three times, showed MacArthur could stand the heat of battle with the best.

After the war he served as superintendent of West Point and then in the Philippines. In 1930 he was appointed the army chief of staff, becoming the youngest officer to ever hold that esteemed position. Eleven years later President Franklin Roosevelt named him as commander of U.S. forces in the Far East, where he helped to organize the feeble American response to Pearl Harbor. Though he failed to hold the Philippines, MacArthur received a Medal of Honor for his actions. He spent the remainder of the war leading forces back toward Tokyo in an im-

mense operation that had the forces hop from one Pacific island to another. On September 2, 1945, he presided at the surrender ceremonies in Tokyo Bay.

The general spent the final years of his life as a chairman of a corporation. He died in 1964.

General Douglas MacArthur (seated in middle) and his commanding officers survey Korea's Inchon harbor.

a mad flight to evade the enemy. "I saw young Americans turn and bolt in battle, or throw down their arms, cursing their government for what they thought was embroilment in a hopeless cause."[15]

Disillusionment with the war bubbled to the surface. As long as the fighting fared well and the United States suffered few casualties, the American public accepted the war as a matter of course. When the conflict dissolved into a bloody mess, people back home, and young soldiers in the field, speedily dropped their enthusiasm.

It was a pattern that would appear often during the Korean War, something that rarely, if ever, happened during World War II. Citizens solidly supported the war effort from 1941 to 1945, whereas support for Korea madly fluctuated as the fortunes of fighting changed and the casualty lists grew longer. The same spirit of sacrifice did not mark the Korean conflict. The veterans of World War II wanted homes, families, and luxuries, and as long as the new war did not become too cumbersome, few criticisms were raised. When the war bogged down, citizens clamored for an end to the fighting and then searched for scapegoats who might bear the blame for the miserable showing.

Some soldiers even wondered why they fought in Korea and failed to see how battle in a distant, miserable land affected the security of their nation. Corporal Stephen Zeg of Chicago said, "I'll fight for my country, but I'll be damned if I see why I'm fighting to save this hell hole."[16] To newspaper readers on the home front, comments like this only reinforced their notion that the country had embarked on a futile mission.

Other factors distanced the American public from the war. South Korea's government, supposedly a democratic organization, was actually ruled by the corrupt dictator Syngman Rhee. Its undisciplined armies hardly posed a threat to North Korea's efficient, well-trained forces backed by weapons from the Soviet Union. One thought occurred to many at home—why send soldiers overseas to fight

Many Americans considered South Korean president Syngman Rhee a corrupt dictator and ill prepared to defend his country.

for such a country, when that country could hardly fight for itself?

Even the esteemed American diplomat Dean Acheson agreed that the nation might not have selected the best location to combat communism. He examined the situation that faced President Truman, then concluded, "If the best minds in the world had set out to find us the worst possible location in the world to fight this damnable war, politically and militarily, the unanimous choice would have been Korea."[17] Some, including President Truman, even wondered if this conflict might spiral into World War III, thereby matching in a titanic clash for world supremacy the forces of democracy, led by the United States, against the forces of communism, led by the Soviet Union.

In a matter of weeks after the UN commitment to Korea, American soldiers had been forced so far back that they battled simply to remain on the Korean peninsula instead of being nudged into the sea. In August 1950, at a place called the Pusan Perimeter in the southeastern edge of Korea, U.S. soldiers dug in, surrounded by the Sea of Japan to the east, the Korea Strait to the south, jagged moun-

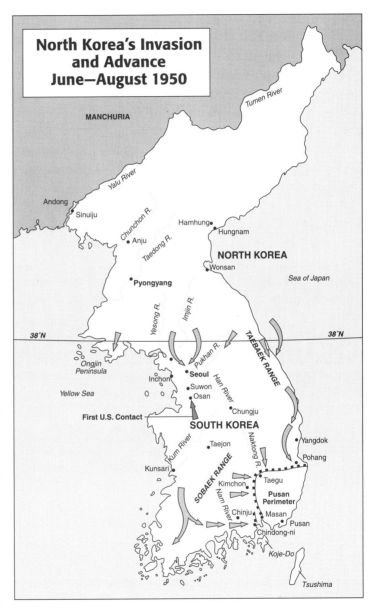

tains to the north, and enemy soldiers stationed to the west. Rather than succumb, though, American soldiers fought desperately for every yard of terrain, held on, and halted the North Korean advance.

"In Heaven's Name, What Are You Doing?"

General Douglas MacArthur reversed the tide by launching an amphibious attack behind enemy lines on September 15. The assault so completely fooled the North Koreans that they either quickly fell back toward the thirty-eighth parallel or surrendered in large numbers. MacArthur's troops continued to shove the foe backward and refused to halt even when it reached the borders at the thirty-eighth parallel. Continuing on like a vast steamroller, American and other allied forces put together by the United Nations raced deep into North Korea toward the Yalu River, the border separating North Korea and China. MacArthur felt so confident of victory that on November 24, 1950, he told reporters, "The war very definitely is coming to an end shortly." [18]

Taking a cue from the commander, the American home front reacted with glee to the news. Whereas only a few short days before they had been ready to abandon the effort, the American public now exulted in the hopes that the war would be over by Christmas. Feats on the battlefield produced praise at home, just as earlier fumbles had received criticism. The home front remained solidly behind the war effort—as long as the prospects for a quick victory appeared good. As of November 24, they looked very good indeed.

That optimism lasted only two days. On November 26, thirty-three divisions of Communist Chinese troops crossed the Yalu and hit American lines with a vengeance. Mac-Arthur had dismissed the notion that the Chinese would intervene, but now he found his forces, apparently on the verge of victory only two days before, reeling backward in disarray before an overwhelming Chinese invasion.

Back at home, dismayed Americans realized that with the addition of the Chinese to the picture, the Korean War would not be the hoped-for speedy win. More than 50 percent believed that the Chinese commitment signaled the initial steps leading to World War III. The elation of one week dissolved under the new state of affairs as men and women again tried to deal with the prospect of enduring a lengthy conflict only five years after they had wrapped up the previous one.

The Korean War turned into a bitter stalemate as the new year approached. American forces answered Chinese advances with well-planned strikes of their own, but neither side made significant gains. The longer the war dragged on, and the higher the casualties mounted, the more bitter the American public reacted to the war. *Stalemate* was not in the U.S. military vocabulary. Americans hit hard, hit fast, finish the job, and walk away with a victory. That was not the case in Korea.

Republicans, eager to once again claim the presidency for their party after years of Democratic occupancy, pounced on Truman. They made clear that, although they supported the war effort and the soldiers in the field, they disagreed with Truman's handling of it. They believed he should commit more troops and finish the job. A beleaguered president received such intense criticism, from both the Republican Party as well as from the public, that he later claimed that November and December 1950 were the worst months of his presidency.

Republican dissatisfaction mirrored the national temper. Senator Joseph McCarthy, a bitter foe of Truman, argued that the fault lay in part with the administration's decision not to build up the military after World War II. McCarthy stated with harsh words, "The Korean death trap we can lay at the doors of the Kremlin [Moscow] and those who sabotaged rearming, including [Secretary of State Dean] Acheson and the President, if you please." [19] *Time* magazine referred to the possibility of Communists working from within the administration.

Truman did not help his cause by announcing that the use of the atom bomb in Korea had been under active consideration. Irate telephone callers tied up the White House phone operators all night with their concerns that an enlarged war could lead to a nuclear holocaust.

During the latter part of 1950, mail to the White House ran twenty to one against the war. One parent wrote to Truman, "I wonder how well you have been sleeping these last nights? Mothers and fathers all over our beloved land are spending sleepless nights worrying again over their boys being sent to fight wars on foreign soil—wars that are no concern of ours." Another person took the president to task as if he

were a youngster. "In heaven's name, what are you doing?" asked the letter writer. "The blood hasn't dried from World War 2. . . . We have nothing to do with Korea. These people are capable of settling their own affairs." [20]

Truman's War

A distinguishing feature of World War II was the amount of change and sacrifice endured by the home front. Ration books limited the amount of meat, sugar, and other food that people could purchase; rubber remained in critically short supply; and steel and tin drives encouraged people to collect those precious commodities for government use.

"I Felt So Utterly Helpless"

Seventeen-year-old marine private Robert Hammond battled in the brutal December 1950 combat near the Chosin Reservoir, where he and 18,000 American army and marine forces found themselves surrounded by 120,000 enemy troops. The predictable outcome left the American lines in tatters. After the battle, Hammond wrote a letter to his father in which he described some of the fighting. The letter is reprinted in Andrew Carroll's 2001 book *War Letters*:

"Three days and nights of bitter fighting went on with heavy losses on both sides. We were outnumbered 10 to 1. We were also trapped and surrounded. I watched a good buddy of mine die of wounds and lack of medicine. I cried, I felt so utterly helpless. . . . Out of 1,400 men we had, just 400 got back. A Battery [Hammond's unit] had 180 men. We now have 42—32 are wounded."

Reflective of the home front's attitude that the Korean War did not justify the same firm support people had given during World War II, little material sacrifice was demanded of the public. The government never turned to rationing, and although it listed some products as priority items for the military, few Americans suffered as a result. A small percentage of citizens hoarded sugar or other items at the war's outset in case the government an-nounced strict measures, and one company added whale meat to its cafeteria menu in case beef became too expensive, but otherwise life went on as usual for the home front.

The most severe restriction that Truman enacted was to place into effect wage and

Tires wait to be recycled during World War II. During the Korean War, the American public was not asked to make material sacrifices.

price controls in January 1951 to bring a measure of stability to the U.S. economy, and even this relatively mild move produced a harsh reaction from many citizens. Some derisively labeled Korea "Truman's War," an epithet toward a leader in wartime that would have been unthinkable during World War II.

President Truman had been attempting to push through Congress a series of measures that would establish public housing for low-income families and set up a system of health care, but the cost of running the war placed this agenda, which he called the Fair Deal, on hold. The threat of communism at home and abroad demanded his attention, and instead of putting money into domestic programs, he tripled the defense budget from $14 billion to $43 billion in one year.

As usually occurs during a conflict, the cost of operating a war fueled the economy. More jobs than ever became available, and the number of people without work plunged to record low levels. So few people remained unemployed in New York that, ironically, the state government had to lay off five hundred workers in its unemployment compensation division.

The major economic concern that Truman faced on the home front unfolded on April 8, 1952, when he seized control of steel plants to avoid a costly strike by steelworkers. The laborers threatened to strike on April 8 unless the steel companies agreed to higher wages, but Truman was concerned over the effect this could have on the war effort and intervened.

His action met immediate opposition from both the steelworkers and the steel companies. The workers claimed his seizure violated their rights to a decent living, and the companies resented government intrusion into what they considered a private concern. Truman believed that, as commander in chief of the armed forces, he had the right to take this step to guarantee the safety of the men fighting in Korea. The court system disagreed. When the issue came before the Supreme Court, the judges issued a six-to-three vote finding the president's action unconstitutional. The strike quickly commenced and lasted seven weeks before an agreement was finally reached.

Scandals

While the fighting raged in Korea, a series of scandals rocked the home front and contributed to the general feeling of insecurity and distrust that marked the era. To many Americans in the first half of the 1950s, it seemed that things changed too quickly, that old ways and trusted methods suddenly could no longer be counted on. Few such crises erupted during World War II, but as was true in many other ways, as far as the home front was concerned, Korea and World War II stood on different levels.

The United States suffered one blow to its sense of stability in May 1950, when the U.S. Senate started investigating organized crime in the country. The Special Committee to Investigate Organized Crime in Interstate Commerce—labeled the Kefauver

Committee after its chairman, Senator Estes Kefauver from Tennessee—called reputed underworld figures to the witness stand and, in front of television cameras that spread the drama live to a captivated nation, discovered how widespread was organized crime's reach. The public was fascinated by this rare glimpse into the shady world of crime yet repelled that such a heinous operation could have tentacles stretching into what appeared every corner of American society.

Senator Kefauver and his committee grilled witnesses for hours, including Frank Costello, the reputed head of organized crime, and William O'Dwyer, the former mayor of New York City. O'Dwyer admitted knowing Costello and appointing to public office friends of figures in organized crime, but he justified it as necessary for properly running the city. Testimony by other witnesses indicated that the New York City Police Department had unspoken agreements not to actively pursue underworld figures.

If certain segments of police departments, politicians, and businesses had ties to crime, who else might be involved, wondered many across the land. Was nothing—family, integrity, honor, security—safe anymore?

Scandal threatened the integrity of college sports in 1951 when the basketball team of City College of New York, a team that had won two consecutive national championships, was implicated in a vast scam to alter the outcome of games. Three of the five starting players accepted bribes to purposely play poorly and lose games.

This example of the nation's younger generation willingly breaking the law to gain money was quickly followed by a disgrace that hit one of the most revered institutions in the land—the U.S. military academy at West Point. For years the complex had molded generations of leaders for the U.S. Army, based on the code of honor and integrity. That code suffered a blow in 1951, however, when ninety students, called cadets, were expelled for cheating on examinations. After reeling in surprise at the college basketball scandal, the nation now had to read details implicating a group of young men whom most people had considered the champions of American honor and values.

An uneasiness swept across the country that nothing was the same anymore and that little could be trusted. Every opportunity to boast of American know-how or moral integrity seemed to be deflated by subsequent scandal. The people on the home front during World War II faced a clear-cut enemy outside their borders—Germany and Japan—and rarely had to fret over threats from within. The Korean War offered no simple picture, however. In addition to being challenged on the Korean battlefields, citizens saw their way of life at home assaulted from all angles.

A Mood of Uncertainty

Respected journalist George Creel wrote of the prevalent feeling in the spring of 1951. "I have never seen anything like it in all my seventy-four years. On any problem it's like

J. Edgar Hoover

J. Edgar Hoover, the director of the Federal Bureau of Investigation (FBI) in the fifties gained a reputation for doggedly pursuing enemies of the nation. Born January 1, 1895, in Washington, D.C., Hoover earned a law degree from George Washington University. In 1917, as an assistant to the U.S. attorney general during World War I, Hoover participated in controversial government raids against groups of suspected traitors. Seven years later Hoover became the director of the FBI, a position he held until his death in 1972.

Hoover modernized the FBI and turned it into an efficient law enforcement agency. In the 1930s, he gained national attention and acclaim for the FBI's campaign against gangsters. He focused the FBI's energies toward communism during the next two decades.

Through the years, Hoover accumulated increasing power, which he had no qualms in using to crush those he thought tried to subvert the United States or against individuals who opposed him. In the 1960s he ordered field agents to track Martin Luther King Jr., a man he despised as arrogant and sexually immoral. Hoover even permitted the use of illegal wiretaps on telephones.

After forty-eight years of running the FBI, Hoover died on May 2, 1972.

FBI director J. Edgar Hoover was infamous for aggressively pursuing enemies of the United States.

those damned hills of Korea. You march up them but there's always the sinking feeling you are going to have to march right back down again."[21]

The frustration levels magnified because Americans saw no way out of the morass at home and abroad. Difficult times can be endured as long as a solution hovers on the horizon, but when no remedy exists, fears, suspicions, and doubts linger.

The prestigious advertising firm of Young and Rubicam placed a statement in every New York newspaper during the Kefauver hearings that reflected the national mood of uncertainty.

> With staggering impact, the telecasts of the Kefauver investigation have brought a shocked awakening to millions of Americans.
>
> Across their television tubes have paraded the honest and dishonest, the frank and the furtive, the public servant and the public thief. Out of many pictures has come a broader picture of the sordid intermingling of crime and politics, of dishonor in public life.
>
> And suddenly millions of Americans are asking:
>
> What's happened to our ideals of right and wrong?
>
> What's happened to our principles of honesty in government?
>
> What's happened to public and private standards of morality?
>
> Then they ask the most important question of all: How can we stop what's going on? Is there anything we can do about it?[22]

Americans across the land nodded their heads in eager yet futile agreement. They did not realize that their frustrations would only intensify in the coming months.

Chapter 3

Conducting an Unpopular War

News from Korea, where American military reverses and successes alternated almost monthly, failed to calm the nation's nerves. For most men and women on the home front, the war had already dragged on far too long, a war against what some saw as a minor Asian power that lacked an atomic arsenal. Something had to be seriously wrong if the nation's armed forces could not readily handle North Korea.

The emotions that engulfed the public seemed to be epitomized in the drama that unfolded among the country's two presidents during the Korean War and the top military commander in Korea, Douglas MacArthur. At first, the home front rallied behind the World War II hero General MacArthur, who they believed would again lead the United States to victory. The general's aggressive strategy and an insubordinate stance toward his superior, President Truman, produced a controversy that split the public even further. The nation's fears that all was not well in Korea rocketed with the alarming news that President Truman had removed General MacArthur from his post. Never in World War II had a president removed his top military commander. One had to look back to the Civil War and Abraham Lincoln for such a precedent—another time when the country was being pulled apart by conflicting passions. Support declined to a precipitous low, helped oust Truman from office, and prodded his successor, Dwight D. Eisenhower, into ending the unpopular conflict.

A Harsh Charge

A clash between Truman and MacArthur had been building for months. The general's arrogance about his military genius had been evident from his earliest days in the army. He considered Truman, who had served as an artillery captain in World War I, as a second-rate officer who should rely on a general's judgment in the war. MacArthur favored bombing targets in China and utilizing the atom bomb, if necessary, as a way of speeding up the war. Truman ignored those proposals, as did most of his top military advisers on the Joint Chiefs of Staff, in hopes that a political arrangement could bring about peace rather than resorting to atomic warfare.

MacArthur countered that since he could not use every weapon at his disposal, his conduct of the war had been impeded by a militarily ignorant president. He told the *U.S. News & World Report* in December 1950 that Truman's limitations were an "enormous handicap, without precedent in military history."[23]

General MacArthur shakes hands with President Truman. Truman relieved MacArthur of his post as military commander in Korea in 1951.

The End of MacArthur

President Truman's dismissal of General MacArthur created a storm of reaction, for and against the move. As one of World War II's most illustrious heroes, MacArthur enjoyed considerable respect in and out of the military. Truman also had his supporters. That caused a flurry of statements throughout the nation. The following quotes were compiled for Time-Life's 1970 publication *This Fabulous Century: 1950–1960*.

> *President Harry S. Truman:* "I believe we must try to limit the war to Korea for these vital reasons: to make sure that the precious lives of our fighting men are not wasted; to see that the security of our country and the free world is not needlessly jeopardized; and to prevent a third world war.

A number of events have made it evident that General MacArthur did not agree with that policy. I have therefore considered it essential to relieve General MacArthur so that there would be no doubt or confusion as to the real purpose and aim of our policy."

Senator Richard M. Nixon: "President Truman has given [the Communists] just what they were after—MacArthur's scalp."

Mrs. Eleanor Roosevelt: "I do not think a general should make policies."

Senator William Jenner: "Our only choice is to impeach President Truman."

MacArthur continued to pester Washington for permission to widen the war. He frequently handed quotes to the press that Truman considered insubordinate, and MacArthur decried his lack of authority to do what he considered necessary to achieve victory.

Truman became so concerned that he might have to relieve the popular general that he dispatched a member of his staff to the Library of Congress to research the episode during the Civil War when Abraham Lincoln had had to dismiss his top military leader, General George McClellan. When Truman examined his aide's notes on the Lincoln-McClellan affair, he realized that the Civil War president, famous for exhibiting patience in difficult moments and giving an individual every chance to act properly, finally felt compelled to replace General McClellan. Truman believed that he had been

equally patient with General MacArthur and had nothing positive to show for it. Truman concluded he had little choice but to remove the aggravating man from his post.

The crisis reached a climax on April 5, 1951. In February, House minority leader Joseph Martin had brutally criticized President Truman in a statement that reflected the views of those on the home front who felt the country should go all out in its effort to deal with the enemy. "What are we in Korea for—to win or to lose?" asked the Republican representative. "If we are not in Korea to win, then this administration should be indicted for the murder of American boys."[24]

A charge as harsh as this—Martin, in effect, had called the president a murderer—was bad enough when coming from the opposition party, but when on April 5 MacArthur announced his agreement with Martin's sentiments, Truman exploded in anger.

He could not allow a subordinate officer to so publicly malign the president. After lining up the support of his Joint Chiefs of Staff, Truman fired MacArthur, even though he realized many citizens at home would castigate him for the move. MacArthur had been their hope for producing a quick victory over the Communists, and his removal would be sure to further enrage a public already worried over what was fast becoming a messy situation in Korea.

"Old Soldiers Never Die"

"Truman Fires MacArthur" read headlines in hundreds of newspapers across the United States on April 11. The nation reacted with disbelief that such a prominent military figure could be removed. Groups of impassioned citizens hanged Truman in effigy in a number of cities, and businesses lowered their flags to half-mast. Some senators talked of impeaching Truman; Senator Joseph McCarthy wondered if Truman had been drunk when making his decision, and Senator Richard Nixon demanded MacArthur's immediate reinstatement. Senator William E. Jenner stated on the floor of the Senate that not only must Congress impeach Truman, but it also must launch an in-depth investigation into whether Communist secret agents in the government had influenced the president.

Two thousand New York longshoremen walked off their jobs in a show of sympathy for the fallen general. A Protestant minister in Texas, irate over MacArthur's firing, died of a heart attack incurred while dictating a harsh message to the president. Letters and telegrams to the White House, delivered by Western Union messengers lugging bushel baskets, ran twenty to one against Truman, and a Gallup poll divulged that 69 percent of Americans sided with MacArthur while a paltry 29 percent leaned toward Truman.

The *Chicago Tribune,* long a bitter critic of Truman, blazoned a front-page piece demanding Truman's removal rather than MacArthur's. "President Truman must be impeached and convicted," ran the editorial. "His hasty and vindictive removal of Gen. MacArthur is the culmination of a series of acts which have shown that he is unfit, morally and mentally, for his high office. The American nation has never been in a greater danger. It is led by a fool who is surrounded by knaves."[25]

A handful of newspapers supported President Truman for doing what a commander in chief had to do—set wartime policy, then make sure everyone followed it. As MacArthur's superior, Truman bore the responsibility of directing the war, and MacArthur's actions challenged that chain of command. The *New York Herald-Tribune,* for instance, praised Truman for acting swiftly to remove a problem that could only have made the situation worse.

The fervor for MacArthur bubbled over when the dismissed commander returned to the United States. Cities organized parades, and dignitaries greeted him with warm words. Such an immense crowd gathered along San Francisco's streets to welcome MacArthur that it took his motorcade two hours to travel a distance of only four-teen miles. A similar parade in Washington, D.C., attracted 300,000 spectators, and 7 million people cheered the hero as he drove through the streets of New York City.

MacArthur added an exclamation point to his popular homecoming with a moving address to Congress, whose members in-terrupted his thirty-four-minute speech on thirty different occasions with loud applause. "I address you with neither rancor nor bitterness in the fading twilight of my life, with but one purpose in mind: To serve

A car carries General MacArthur through downtown San Francisco during a ticker-tape parade.

my country." He added, "Why, my soldiers asked of me, surrender military advantages to an enemy in the field?" He paused for effect, "I could not answer." The general then ended with words that have become famous in American history.

I am closing my fifty-two years of military service. When I joined the Army, even before the turn of the century, it was the fulfillment of all of my boyish hopes and dreams. . . . The hopes and dreams have long since vanished, but I still remember the refrain of one of the most popular barracks ballads of that day, which proclaimed most proudly that old soldiers never die; they just fade away. And like the old soldier of that ballad, I now close my military career and just fade away, an old soldier who tried to do his duty as God gave him the light to see that duty.[26]

In the following days, MacArthur added to the controversy by suggesting that his dismissal, and other disturbing trends in the United States, had been caused by "insidious forces working from within," especially communism. He warned, "We must not underestimate the peril. It must not be brushed off lightly."[27]

Truman Strikes Back

President Truman bided his time while the celebrations for MacArthur unfolded. He wrote that he "was sorry to have to reach a parting of the way with the big man in Asia [MacArthur], but he asked for it and I had to

give it to him." He correctly figured that the nation would wildly welcome home their hero, heap honors and awards on him, and then a few weeks later would turn to other matters and relegate MacArthur to the background. He reassured his staff and the cabinet that in six weeks the nation would turn in his favor: "The American people will come to understand that what I did had to be done."[28]

That is precisely what occurred. Truman gained support when the Joint Chiefs of Staff, who oversaw the nation's military, backed Truman's actions against MacArthur. The general's popularity further declined when congressional hearings into the firing opened on May 3, 1951. After MacArthur testified for three days, pro-administration witnesses presented the government's side. Secretary of Defense George C. Marshall began by stating how difficult it was for him, a career military man, to criticize another officer whom he had known for so long. He called it "a very distressing necessity, a very distressing occasion that compels me to appear here this morning and in effect in almost direct opposition to a great many views and actions of General MacArthur. He is a brother Army officer, a man for whom I have tremendous respect."[29] Marshall then claimed that MacArthur badly overstepped his authority in publicly criticizing the president.

The chairman of the Joint Chiefs of Staff, Omar Bradley, swerved public opinion more by bluntly stating that MacArthur's proposals for broadening the war would have forced China to enter. That, Bradley emphasized, would have been the "wrong war, at the

General George C. Marshall believed Truman's actions against MacArthur were justified.

wrong place, at the wrong time, and with the wrong enemy."[30]

Gradually, the public turned away from MacArthur. Some people understood the correctness of what Truman had done, but others simply became wrapped up in more important issues. However, a bitter taste lingered. The affair marked one more item in a string of events that had disrupted the American home front.

"I Shall Go to Korea"

As the war dragged on in Korea with no apparent victory in sight, Truman's ratings continued to decline. His approval rating plunged to a new low of 26 percent in early 1952, and Truman received so much criticism that one newspaper thought it necessary to remind its readers that, "after all, the President of the United States is a member of the human race."[31]

Americans had just about reached the end of their patience with the war. To date, the United States had carried most of the war's burden, both in soldiers committed and funds allocated, and the United Nations supplied the rest. Of the 520,000 troops sent to assist the South Korean forces from the war's outset, 90 percent were from the United States. People at home wondered why the country should risk so many soldiers and expend such vast sums of money when the rest of the world would only contribute 50,000 soldiers. The United States seemed to be fighting for a nation that suffered from a corrupt government and ill-disciplined soldiers of its own. With public opinion running so strongly against him, on March 29, 1952, President Truman announced that he would not seek reelection for another term as president in the fall elections.

A mad scramble ensued in which both parties pushed forward their candidates to replace Truman. The Republicans, who had not controlled the presidency since 1933, the year Franklin D. Roosevelt took office, saw their chance to again sweep into power. After years of tumultuous events

Dwight D. Eisenhower visits Korea. Shortly after taking office, Eisenhower negotiated an agreement to end the war.

and controversies, the Republicans turned to the one man they thought could unite the American people—Dwight D. Eisenhower. The likeable Eisenhower had earned everyone's respect for commanding all Allied forces in Europe in the momentous victory over Nazism. His calm demeanor and fatherly image seemed perfectly suited for a nation in turmoil over events both overseas and at home. Eisenhower's opponent, Democrat Adlai Stevenson of Illinois, stood at a distinct disadvantage, even though he was respected for his humor and intelligence.

Eisenhower quickly took advantage of the public's disillusion with Korea. On October 24, 1952, he stated in a nationally tele-

vised speech in Detroit, Michigan, that if elected, he would travel to Korea to end the war. "The job [presidency] requires a personal trip to Korea. I shall make that trip. Only in that way could I learn best how to serve the American people in the cause of peace. I shall go to Korea."[32]

Eisenhower never made it clear whether he intended to end the war militarily or diplomatically, but the prospect of the revered warrior resolving the situation appealed to the country. On election day 1952, voters overwhelmingly elected Eisenhower to be the next president.

Eisenhower, nicknamed "Ike," kept his promise. On November 29, 1952, before assuming the office of presidency in January 1953, Eisenhower secretly traveled to Korea. While an arranged roster of dignitaries purposely visited Eisenhower's empty New York apartment to make it appear he was still there, the president-elect spent three days visiting the troops at the fighting front to learn firsthand the situation. After listening to the men in the field and their commanding officers, Eisenhower concluded that the United States faced only a few options to end the war—either widen it through use of the atom bomb, which he dismissed, or attempt to negotiate a settlement that would return both North and South Korea to their prewar borders. He refused to permit the war, with its accompanying casualties, to drag on, so he decided that once in office he would place his efforts into a negotiated peace.

"There Was No Rejoicing"

Eisenhower moved quickly after being sworn in as president. He encouraged the South Korean government to expand its armed forces to more than half a million so that the burden of conducting the war could gradually be eased from the United States. He also instructed his negotiators in Korea to reach an agreement with the enemy as soon as possible.

Within a few months Eisenhower had his wish. On July 27, 1953, more than three years after the war's opening, negotiators reached a settlement that returned Korea to the conditions existing before the war.

Dwight D. Eisenhower

Born in Texas in 1890 but growing up in Abilene, Kansas, Dwight D. Eisenhower turned a stellar military career into a two-term presidency during the 1950s. He excelled in both sports and academics in high school, then attended West Point to become an army officer.

He served under some of the army's top-ranking officers, including Generals John J. Pershing in Mexico and Europe and Douglas MacArthur in the Philippines. When World War II broke out, he commanded Allied forces that landed in North Africa in late 1942 as a prelude to his major assignment. President Franklin D. Roosevelt selected the quiet man to lead the gigantic Allied assault on France in June 1944. A successful, though bloody, landing in Normandy led to an eleven-month campaign during which troops under Eisen-

hower steadily shoved German leader Adolf Hitler's forces back inside the German borders.

Victory in Europe thrust Eisenhower to the top of both political parties' list as presidential material. As the Republican nominee in 1952, he triumphed over the Democrats, then served for eight years as chief executive. Though suffering a heart attack in September 1955, Eisenhower returned in time to win reelection. One of the most momentous actions of his second term occurred in 1957, when he dispatched soldiers to Little Rock, Arkansas, to guarantee the right of nine African American students to attend the previously all-white Central High School.

Eisenhower retired to Gettysburg, Pennsylvania, in 1961. He died on March 28, 1969, after a lengthy illness.

When the truce became public on July 27, 1953, little rejoicing occurred in the United States. People erupted in a frenzy of celebration at the end of World War II, but now all that most people wanted was a return to normalcy. The war, never popular with the public after the first few months, faded from view as men and women turned their attention to families and jobs.

Those who celebrated the cease of hostilities did so more out of relief than exultation in the outcome. The United States could claim no clearcut victory here; the North Koreans had only been confined to their prewar borders, where they still, as

American troops in Korea celebrate the truce ending the war.

Communists, remained a threat to the democratic world. Americans took solace only in knowing that the killing had halted.

"I was happy it was over," declared General Arthur Trudeau, the commander of the U.S. Army's Seventh Division. "It was apparent that all we were going to do was sit there and hold positions. There wasn't going to be any victory. All we could do was go on losing more lives."[33]

The prevalent opinion, in both the military in Korea and the civilians on the home front, was relief that the nation could forget about the war and move on to other considerations. Lieutenant Clyde Fore of the Twenty-seventh Infantry Division said, "There was no rejoicing—we were just sad and quiet. This was the first time Americans had ever accepted a no-win war. To me, Korea had been an abomination. So many people had died, for what?"[34]

The casualties in a conflict that produced neither gains nor triumphs staggered analysts. The United States lost 33,629 dead and another 105,785 wounded. A poll taken right after the end of the fighting showed that 62 percent of the American public believed the war had not been worth fighting.

Nothing Changed

The end of hostilities in Korea differed from the experience of World War II in another way. In 1945, after the armed forces had defeated Germany and Japan, the country pulled back to within its own borders with a confidence bred of victory. The nation had dismantled its opponent and removed the main threats to peace.

That was not the case following Korea. Instead of removing a peril, the war had only returned the situation to what had existed in 1950. Communism still lurked overseas, and people, without saying so, understood that one day the nation might again have to grapple with that foe.

A newer element elevated Americans' concern that the world they now faced presented a roster of uncertainties. President Eisenhower spoke not only of the enemy across the seas but also those that undermined the country from within. On national television, President Eisenhower reminded the American people that although the battlefields in Korea may have fallen silent, the nation still had to be vigilant against Communist spies and saboteurs inside the borders. He stated that the United States had not gained "peace in the world. We may not now relax our guard nor cease our quest."[35]

The thought that sinister agents lurked on street corners or worked from inside the government created a mood of distrust. Instead of returning to their jobs and homes content with war's end, the home front still had to deal with lingering challenges to its way of life. The Korean War may have ended on the military front, but the home front still had its battles to fight.

Chapter 4

Senator Joseph McCarthy and the Red Scare

Turmoil at home from the Korean War commenced long before the war ended. Suspicions of Communist spies in the country had actually started during World War II, but the climate of fear and distrust multiplied with combat in Korea. A "Red Scare," a national apprehension that Communist agents actively worked to produce the overthrow of the government and that dangerous enemies lurked in every corner, created a paranoia that led to suppressive steps, some of which violated constitutional rights. It did not take long for someone to take advantage of this national mood and orchestrate an immense campaign to purge the United States of foreign menaces.

Cold War Spies

A series of spy cases sapped Americans' confidence that they were safe behind their borders. The U.S. government indicted, and later convicted, eleven leaders of the Communist Party of the United States with con-

spiracy to overthrow the government. In January 1950, after a lengthy investigation, a high government official, Alger Hiss, was convicted of perjury. He had been accused of being a Communist spy and delivering secrets to the Soviet Union.

A similar case in Great Britain made people wonder if any secrets were safe from the Communists. In February 1950 the British government announced the arrest of Klaus Fuchs, a scientist who had worked on the top-secret atom bomb project in New Mexico for the United States. If the Soviet Union placed spies inside the super-secret atom bomb program, where else in government might Communist agents be located?

Authorities arrested two Americans in conjunction with the Fuchs case—Ethel and Julius Rosenberg. The government charged the couple, members of the American Communist Party, with conspiring to convey secret information to the Soviet Union. Although the evidence seemed weak, in the climate of the times, the pair received the death sentence. The couple perished in the electric chair on June 19, 1953.

The Search for Communists

The cumulative effect of these events produced greater fear at home and an increased desire for government scrutiny over suspicious individuals. People needed

someone to blame for the rise of communism and for the threat it now posed. They wanted to vent their annoyance because, instead of enjoying newfound prosperity and peace at home after winning World

FBI agents arrest Julius Rosenberg (center) for spying. Rosenberg and his wife Ethel were executed in 1953.

War II, American citizens still had to worry about their security.

It is hardly surprising that in such a climate of fear, a government investigative committee with authority over domestic matters acted with impunity. The House Un-American Activities Committee (HUAC) received the task from the House of Rep-resentatives of investigating "all entities, groups or individuals who are alleged to advise, teach or advocate the overthrow by force or violence the Government of the United States."[36] The committee looked into hundreds of allegations, many hardly more than rumor and suspicion.

A Lost Sense of Humor

One victim of the national paranoia that marked the hunt for Communists in the country was acclaimed movie comedian Charlie Chaplin, who, because of his criticism of the government, was refused reentry into the country after visiting his homeland, Great Britain. Instead of fighting the action, Chaplin lived the remainder of his years in Europe.

Citizens reacted in a variety of ways, from support of the action to outright condemnation. Contemporary news columnist I.F. Stone voiced what many of his colleagues felt in an April 25, 1953, column that was reprinted in his 1963 book *The Haunted Fifties.*

There must be something seriously wrong with our America if Chaplin could no longer live in it. He [Chaplin] never became an American citizen but Charlie Chaplin was and will remain more truly American than the blackguards and fanatics who hounded him, the cheap politicians who warned him not to come back.

We do not blame Charlie Chaplin for leaving us. Who could blame a comic genius—one of the greatest of all time—for being unwilling to live in a country which seems to have lost its sense of humor?

Stone had one final request of the comedian who made America laugh for so long. He urged him to make a film about 1950s America similar to the satirical one he produced about Adolf Hitler.

"Turn the laugh on them [McCarthy and his followers], Charlie, for our country's sake. This capital [Washington, D.C.,] needs nothing so badly as one final well-flung custard pie."

Charlie Chaplin was not allowed to return to the United States after criticizing the American government.

Accusations against those in the movie industry gained widespread press. Hollywood had always been viewed as very liberal and somewhat licentious. Many actors, directors, and writers refused to testify about their political beliefs or about those of their coworkers. As a result, because of their "suspicious" activities, which included membership in unions urging radical change or in groups that openly espoused communism, certain individuals were blacklisted—their names placed on a list of those that no Hollywood studio would hire out of fear of being labeled soft on communism. Although some careers sank due to the HUAC hearings, others rose. Richard Nixon, who later became president of the United States, fashioned his political career on the basis of his work with the committee.

In the United States during the early 1950s, some people imagined spies lurking in every corner, a feeling that was heightened during the war against communism in Korea. In 1950, a Houston, Texas, couple entered a Chinese restaurant to obtain help from the owners for a research project. When another customer overheard the group chatting in Chinese, the individual telephoned the police with the complaint that the people were secretly discussing communism in an Asian tongue and should be arrested. Police quickly arrived, took the couple away, and held them for fourteen hours before deciding they had done nothing wrong.

"Beware, Commies, Spies, Traitors"

The Korean War had one similarity with World War II with regards to the home front—it yielded a stream of books and magazines dealing with the conflict. Many of them became immensely popular as a result. Literature of all sorts, from novels to comic books, urged Americans to be on the lookout for infiltrators and spies and warned Communists that they faced defeat. Mickey Spillane, the author of the immensely popular Mike Hammer detective series, pitted his fictional hero against Communists more frequently than he did against murderers and thieves. In his 1951 book *One Lonely Night*, which sold 3 million copies, Spillane has Mike Hammer boast,

> I killed more people tonight than I have fingers on my hands. I shot them in cold blood and enjoyed every minute of it. I pumped slugs in the nastiest bunch of bastards you ever saw. . . . They were Commies. . . . They were red sons-of-bitches who should have died long ago. . . . They never thought there were people like me in this country. They figured us all to be soft as horse manure and just as stupid. [37]

To influence the impressionable youth of the country, Marvel comic-book hero Captain America warned Communists, "Beware, commies, spies, traitors, and foreign agents! Captain America, with all loyal, free men behind him, is looking for you, ready to fight until the last one of you is exposed for the yellow scum you are." [38]

Even trading cards carried warnings and information about communism. One card bore the drawing of a typical American city with billowing atomic bomb clouds approaching from the background. Smiling from his vantage point in the clouds was the Grim Reaper. Underneath were the words, "But an America fully prepared to defend itself is not likely to be attacked. The Reds understand this language." Below this phrase, in bolder letters, stated, "FIGHT THE RED MENACE."[39]

"I Have Here in My Hand"

On February 9, 1950, Wisconsin senator Joseph McCarthy delivered a speech in Wheeling, West Virginia, commemorating Abraham Lincoln's birthday. The politician warned of an internal threat to the security of the United States and casually inserted into his text that Communists in the State Department in Washington, D.C., profoundly influenced foreign policy.

"While I cannot take the time to name all the men in the State Department who have been named as members of the Communist Party and members of a spy ring," McCarthy declared, "I have here in my hand a list of 205 that were known to the Secretary of State as being members of the Communist Party and who nevertheless are still working and shaping the policy of the State Department."[40]

The senator did not suspect that his charges would create much reaction. Then he flew to a press conference in Denver, Colorado, where eager newspaper reporters surrounded McCarthy and queried him about the list. When they asked if he could produce the piece of paper holding the 205 names, Senator McCarthy claimed that he had left it in the pocket of a suit still in his suitcase. The press accepted the excuse, and not one reporter challenged the senator to mention specific names.

A Climate of Fear

The Wisconsin Republican took advantage of the fear and paranoia that swept across the nation in the years following World War II. Citizens witnessed the spread of communism throughout Eastern Europe and Asia and wondered what evil conspiracy lay behind it. In the wake of trials convicting Americans as being Communist spies, people turned their gazes inward and asked if foreign agents could be at work trying to undermine the very principles of the United States.

This climate produced intense anxiety at home before and during the Korean War. Americans experienced a new vulnerability against which even the immense oceans could not protect them. If a Soviet atom or hydrogen bomb did not reach their shores, certainly sinister agents and saboteurs, eager to construct a Communist regime on the ruins of an American democracy, labored to destroy a system of government that had been laboriously honed for almost two hundred years. Whereas the major threats to American security had always existed overseas, this time the menace lurked inside the country's borders. Americans could no longer feel safe—agents of destruction might exist anywhere.

Senator McCarthy knew how to use this mood to advance his cause. After the Wheeling speech, he purposely announced subsequent charges against government workers in smaller towns, where he could avoid intense scrutiny from an established press. The town might have only a local Associated Press representative who, without thoroughly checking the charges, would send the information across the wires. McCarthy also knew that the press faced deadlines, so he waited to make a statement until shortly before deadlines so that reporters had little time to verify his charges.

The Newsworthy Senator

McCarthy won elections when many Republicans did not, so the Republican Party turned a blind eye to his frequent use of unsubstantiated charges and character as-

sassinations. In their quest to regain power, prominent Republican politicians and supporters were not about to toss aside a man who, although unscrupulous, defeated the Democrats. They therefore said little when McCarthy attacked the Truman administration for shielding a haven of Communist spies.

The press was also not about to abandon someone who so frequently delivered potent quotes. Instead of being a bland politician who uttered forgettable phrases, McCarthy dished out vivid sentences. A reporter could write stories about the flamboyant McCarthy on almost a daily basis. William Edwards, a reporter who followed McCarthy around the

Senator Joseph McCarthy tells the Senate Foreign Relations Subcommittee that Communists have infiltrated the State Department.

country for the *Chicago Tribune,* said, "McCarthy was a dream story. I wasn't off page one for four years."[41]

McCarthy's bluster and his bold manner of attacking those who disagreed with him kept detractors at a distance. Many national reporters failed to adequately check on his background or to conduct their own investigations into the senator's charges, and they conveniently overlooked McCarthy's penchant for alcohol.

A "Campaign of Half-Truths and Untruths"

Handling McCarthy with kid gloves continued as long as he issued statements like that of June 14, 1951. During a speech delivered on the Senate floor, he spoke of Communists burrowing into the United States from inside and claimed that there existed a "conspiracy so immense, an infamy so black, as to dwarf any in the history of man."[42] Reporters, and their reading audiences, found those phrases irresistible.

A few observers raised concerns over the politician's methods when McCarthy lowered the 205 Communists in the State Department to 57, then raised it to 81. If anyone asked him for the list of names, Senator McCarthy always gave a convenient excuse for not having it with him at that moment. Again, eager to wire electrical phrases and sentences across the nation, reporters failed to pursue the discrepancies.

Should they desire to take on the Wisconsin politician, reporters and other politicians need only look at one stark example

of McCarthy's power. The Senate set up an investigative committee to examine McCarthy's charges. Led by Maryland democrat Millard Tydings, the committee scoured documents and interviewed witnesses, but unearthed no evidence of communism inside the government. The committee announced on July 7, 1950, that all of McCarthy's charges had been based on rumors and stated they were nothing more than "a fraud and a hoax. They represent perhaps the most nefarious [evil] campaign of half-truths and untruths in the history of this republic. For the first time in our history, we have seen the totalitarian technique of the 'big lie' employed on a sustained basis."[43]

McCarthy, buttressed by fellow Republican politicians, labeled the report an assault on his integrity that was, itself, built upon lies and rumor. That November, McCarthy openly backed the Republican nominee in the race for the Senate seat currently held by Senator Tydings. In a brutal campaign, McCarthy pulled no punches to defeat the man who conducted the Senate investigation into his affairs. He and his aides handed out doctored photographs that supposedly showed Tydings shaking hands with Earl Browder, the head of the Communist Party in the United States. Although Tydings had never met the man, the photo's impact upon an electorate ready to believe in a Communist conspiracy resulted in defeat for the Democrat.

A Dangerous Time

The mood of the nation, abetted by the fears of world communism's spread and by

open hostility in Korea, led to steps that some hoped would safeguard the nation. Although a few may have been necessary, many actions were little more than hasty reactions to mass hysteria. In 1951, Congress passed the McCarran Internal Security Act, a law that required all known Communists to register with the government. The act also permitted the establishment of camps into which Communists could be confined should the president declare a national emergency. Few were concerned that such camps used in World War II, where they

Congress passed an act to establish internment camps for Communists similar to those used for Japanese Americans during World War II.

housed Japanese Americans, had later come under heavy criticism as violating civil rights. These were different times and different people—citizens orchestrated by international communism, directed by the Soviet Union, and willing to destroy democracy.

Two years later, President Eisenhower issued Executive Order 10450. To help prevent Communists from entering the government,

Dr. J. Robert Oppenheimer (at left) exhibits a picture of the atomic bomb blast over Nagasaki, Japan.

the order instituted a program that investigated all new government workers as well as any employee of a company that chose to deal with the U.S. government. Background checks determined the loyalty of each worker, and anyone with a questionable past became subject to dismissal. Following the government's lead, other institutions in business and industry adopted similar programs.

McCarthy succeeded, in part, because the people welcomed his message. They wanted something done to protect democracy. In times of fear such as existed during the fifties, this attitude often veered toward the absurd. One Hollywood studio canceled plans to make a film about the Native American figure Hiawatha because the main character supposedly wanted to stop wars between warring Indian tribes. The studio executives feared that the public would see

this film as Communist-inspired propaganda that promoted peace with communism.

In a similar vein, a member of the Indiana State Textbook Commission, which regulated the books to be used in the state's public classrooms, questioned the inclusion in school curriculum of the medieval tale concerning Robin Hood. He felt that it glorified stealing from the rich for the benefit of the poor, a Communist theory in this member's opinion.

The State Department joined the act by issuing a directive that banned from the shelves of public libraries books written by Communists or those sympathetic to communism. Librarians struggled with the vagueness of the order. They wondered which authors would be considered Communist sympathizers? To be safe, many librarians removed books, such as the novels of John Steinbeck, that merely dealt with the struggling poor and class antagonism. A handful of librarians even burned suspect literature.

The fear that pervaded the nation clamped down on intellectual thought and questioning. The respected scientist who headed the nation's program to develop the atom bomb in World War II, J. Robert Oppenheimer, had been thoroughly investigated and cleared by the government before receiving the post. When again investigated during the 1950s, the same background information, which indicated that in college he had frequented meetings of groups suspected of having ties to communism, now placed him on the undesirable list. In a 1950 election, Richard Nixon furthered his political career, in part, by labeling his opponent, Helen Gahagan Douglas, "pink down to her underwear."[44]

"Watch the Skies"

The threat of communism that launched McCarthy to his public platform also altered the way Hollywood conducted business during the Korean War. Since the ability of Hollywood to make a film was partially dependent on the financial contributions of businessmen, normally a conservative group, Hollywood executives freely cooperated with HUAC.

Executives read scripts with a more discerning eye for antigovernment statements or story plots that involved revolution. One producer said, "I now read scripts through the eyes of the DAR [Daughters of the American Revolution, a strongly conservative and patriotic organization]. I'm scared to death," he added, "and nobody can tell me it isn't because I'm afraid of being investigated."[45]

As a result, many movies depicted the nation as basically the same—middle class, white, with few major problems. Escapist films like romances and westerns dominated. Those that chose a serious topic focused on one theme—the battle against communism.

Movies, especially science fiction films, tried to mirror the contemporary conflict with communism. The 1951 movie *I Was a Communist for the FBI* presented the story of counter-espionage work against communism, and numerous science fiction films cast the U.S. military, or a group of scientists, against some unnatural peril, often created by radiation from atomic weapons. Just as the U.S. military faced its dangers on the battlefields of Korea and the home front dealt with real and imagined threats from within, so too did Hollywood present its own versions of individuals or the nation facing enemies. *The Beast, The Blob, The Creature from the Black Lagoon*, and *The Thing from Another World* featured immense monsters that threatened to destroy society, just as communism supposedly threatened the nation. *The Invasion of the Body Snatchers* depicted a group of people, hatched in pods, created to look just like "average" Americans. In reality they are threats to civilization who strictly follow orders—like Communists supposedly did. In a remarkable reflection of the paranoia that engulfed the early 1950s, one 1951 film, *The Thing from Another World* even ends with a character warning the audience to "watch the skies . . . watch everywhere . . . keep looking . . . *watch the skies!*" [46] The warning might as easily have been uttered by Senator McCarthy.

"Stop Playing with Fire"

One notable science fiction film burst out of the mold that trapped most in its genre. A spaceship lands on Earth in the 1951 movie *The Day the Earth Stood Still,* but instead of destructive aliens, this one brings a warning of impending doom—not from communism but rather from the nuclear arms race. The main character, an alien named Klaatu, informs world leaders that he has been sent by an advanced civilization to inform the people of Earth that they face annihilation if they do not abandon their weapons. "Don't play with the atomic bomb," he pleads. "You are irresponsible children whose powers exceed your wisdom. Grow up and stop playing with fire." [47] Instead of listening to his advice, the U.S. Army attacks and forces Klaatu to depart.

While television did not offer as wide a selection of anti-Communist programs as did Hollywood, it also contributed its share. The most famous, *I Led Three Lives,* presented the true story of U.S. counterspy Herbert A. Philbrick, whose exploits had been first told in a 1952 book. The series ran for three years, with each episode offering a new Communist challenge for Philbrick. In one episode, the commander of the secret Soviet spy cell that Philbrick has infiltrated makes an unusual request—take in his daughter while he travels out of town on business. Philbrick agrees, then catches the daughter examining his belongings and discussing Communist propaganda with his own daughter. The character, played by actor Richard Carlson, gives the dire warning, "Never underestimate a Commie, even a baby one." [48]

Speaking Out Against McCarthy

Like most trends that sweep over the nation, the mood of doubt and suspicion that elevated Senator Joseph McCarthy eventually weakened enough that critics attacked the once-formidable politician. Supreme Court justice William O. Douglas stated that McCarthy's assaults on Americans endangered free thought. The Catholic weekly *Commonweal* ended an article detailing McCarthy's career by calling him careless, ignorant, and cowardly. *Time* magazine stated that "after nearly two years of tramping the nation, shouting that he was 'rooting out the skunks,' just how many Communists has Joe rooted out? The answer is: none." [49]

Herbert Philbrick, the real counterspy and not his television counterpart, claimed that Communist leaders in the Soviet Union believed McCarthy helped them by spreading a web of fear and distrust to all corners of the United States. The *New York Times* agreed in an editorial, stating, "If a major objective of Russian foreign policy is to undermine the faith of Democratic

No Time to Keep Silent

News reporter Edward R. Murrow shot to prominence during World War II when he electrified radio audiences in the United States with his vivid accounts of life in London, England, under the intense German bombing campaign. He gained a reputation for pulling no punches. Murrow never shied from calling something what it was.

He remained true to that reputation in his broadcasts dealing with Senator Joseph McCarthy. Murrow courageously took a stand against the popular senator's campaign to attack individuals as Communists. In a March 1954 airing of his *See It Now* television program, Murrow muttered words that many in the news industry had long wanted to say but had feared to do so because of McCarthy's frightening power. The words are included in Alexander Kendrick's 1969 biography of Murrow, *Prime Time*.

We will not be driven by fear into an age of unreason, if we dig deep into our own history and our doctrine and remember that we are not descended from fearful men, not from men who feared to write, to speak, to associate, and to defend causes which were for the moment unpopular.

This is no time for men who oppose Senator McCarthy's methods to keep silent. We can deny our heritage and our history, but we cannot escape responsibility for the result. There is no way for a citizen of a republic to abdicate his responsibilities.

Edward R. Murrow took a courageous stand against Senator McCarthy and his Communist smear campaign.

peoples in their governments, then the Kremlin [Moscow] must rejoice every time that Joseph R. McCarthy opens his mouth in the Senate of the United States."[50]

An astonishing sign that people had wearied of McCarthy's incessant attacks occurred when President Eisenhower, who had steadfastly refused to condemn his fellow Republican, finally joined the ranks of those who felt the senator had gone too far. The normally calm Eisenhower compared McCarthy to a pimple that had to be removed, and he also admonished people to avoid extremist acts such as book burnings and bannings. On June 14, 1953, the president said,

> Don't join the book burners. Don't think you are going to conceal faults by concealing evidence that they ever existed. Don't be afraid to go in your library and read every book as long as any document does not offend our own ideas of decency. That should be the only censorship.
>
> How will we defeat communism unless we know what it is? What it teaches— why does it have such an appeal for men? . . . We have got to fight it with something better. Not try to conceal the thinking of our own people. They are part of America and even if they think ideas that are contrary to ours they have a right to have them, a right to record them and a right to have them in places where they are accessible to others. It is unquestioned or it is not America.[51]

Television news reporter Edward R. Murrow hammered another nail in McCarthy's coffin in a February 1954 news documentary. On his program *See It Now,* Murrow, long an ardent advocate of free speech, summarized McCarthy's campaign. The program's anti-McCarthy slant appealed to viewers, as telephone calls to the television studio ran fifteen to one in favor of Murrow's viewpoint.

"Have You No Sense of Decency, Sir?"

The end for the senator from Wisconsin came from another set of government hearings. In 1954 the Senate investigated McCarthy after he had been accused of attempting to gain preferential treatment from the army for an assistant, Private G. David Schine. The hearings, televised nationally, showed McCarthy at his worst. He abused witnesses during his examinations, shouted down opponents' statements, called people names, and utilized his time-honored ploy of verbally attacking anyone who attacked him. McCarthy accused the army of forty-six instances of wrongdoing, then mentioned that he had information that someone involved in the hearings was a Communist.

Lawyer Joseph Welch, representing the U.S. Army, asked McCarthy to divulge the information he possessed about the supposed Communist. McCarthy said,

> I think we should tell him [Welch] that he has in his law firm a young man

named Fisher whom he recommended, incidentally, to do work on this committee, who has been for a number of years a member of an organization which was named, oh, years and years ago, as the legal bulwark of the Communist Party.[52]

Welch, stunned at this accusation against his fellow lawyer, who had as a youth belonged to the Lawyers Guild, quickly gathered his thoughts. As an absorbed nation watched the drama on live television, Welch answered in measured terms that cut the legs out from underneath McCarthy. "Until this moment, Senator, I think I never really gauged your cruelty or your recklessness. Fred Fisher is a young man who went to the Harvard Law School and came into my firm and is starting what looks to be a brilliant career with us."[53]

Welch continued his defense of Fisher, then added,

Little did I dream you could be so reckless and so cruel as to do an injury to that lad. It is true that he is still with Hale & Dorr. It is true that he will continue to be with Hale & Dorr. It is, I regret to say, equally true that I fear he shall always bear a scar needlessly inflicted by you. If it were in my power to forgive you for your reckless cruelty, I would do so. I like to think I am a gentle man, but your forgiveness will have to come from someone other than me.[54]

The lawyer, before a hushed Senate committee, ended with the powerful words, "Let us not assassinate this lad further, Senator. You have done enough. Have you no sense of decency, sir, at long last? Have you

"The Silence of Timid Men"

Reporter Edward R. Murrow not only took Senator McCarthy to task but also directed criticism toward his own industry. He believed the media had kept silent about the senator's reckless charges for too long and in so doing had helped create the spread of McCarthyism throughout the nation.

Five years after airing his McCarthy program, Murrow explained his views in a speech delivered in London, the scene of his riveting radio broadcasts during World War II. The words are reprinted in Alexander Kendrick's 1969 biography of Murrow, *Prime Time.*

His [Senator McCarthy's] weapon was fear. He was a politically unsophisticated man with a flair for publicity, and he was powerfully aided by the silence of timid men who feared to be the subject of his unfounded accusations. He polluted the channels of communication, and every radio and television network, every newspaper and magazine publisher who did not speak out against him, contributed to his evil work and must share responsibility for what he did, not only to our fellow citizens but to our self-respect.

The timidity of television in dealing with this man when he was spreading fear throughout the land is not something to which this art of communication can ever point with pride. Nor should it be allowed to forget it.

left no sense of decency?"[55] The room burst into applause, and even press photographers joined in.

These words resonated through the United States and marked the political end of Joseph McCarthy. It was almost as if the nation, through Welch, cried out that it had had enough after four years of reckless incrimination. On December 2, 1954, the Senate voted sixty-seven to twenty-two to condemn McCarthy. Though he remained in the Senate, without his platform and national support, the politician faded to powerlessness. On May 2, 1957, after years of alcohol abuse, a broken McCarthy died from cirrhosis of the liver.

The nation's growing indifference to Senator McCarthy ended his reign of fear almost as much as Welch's words. The Korean War and the accompanying crusade to uncover supposed Communist agents throughout the country increasingly taxed people's patience. They had waited during World War II to start building their lives, complete with family and home, and they were now eager to again return to a more mundane existence. Businesses and national trends arrived to satisfy their needs.

Chapter 5

A Longing for Complacency and Conformity

In addition to possible Communist spies and the arms race, the Korean War added one more unstable element that society back home had to endure during the early 1950s. Instead of peace and calm, which the home front sorely desired after the tumultuous events of World War II, strife in Korea vied for people's attention.

The American public, unlike in the previous war, tried to suppress thoughts of the conflict by turning to other matters. Battlefield reports and casualty lists might arrive, but Americans had had enough of that during the 1940s. In a negative reaction to the fighting, they instead tried to create what many saw as the ideal world, a world in contrast to the turmoil taking place on the other side of the Pacific—a conflict-free society where conformity, not disruption and chaos, was the norm; a nation where families were happy and prosperous and contented; a place where the American dream of home and cars, new television sets and refrigerators, could be attained. The world might be

torn with Cold War fears and conflict in Korea, but Americans were not about to let that disrupt their daily lives.

"The Family Is the Center of Your Living"

With the longing for calmer times came an increased emphasis on the family unit. Times of chaos and disruption frequently bring with them an opposite tendency for people to more tightly hold on to those aspects of their lives that mean consistency and continuity. Solid families consisting of two parents, a mother who remained home while the father headed to work, provided one answer. The stability and structure offered by family countered the Communist surge that rose in other nations and seemed to be taking aim at America.

Younger people wanted families, and the nation encouraged that desire. A popular book of the time, *The Woman's Guide to Better Living*, stated, "Whether you are a man or a woman, the family is the unit to which you most genuinely belong. The family is the center of your living. If it isn't, you've gone far astray."[56] In a sign that a sense of belonging was important to people on the home front, polls of college girls divulged that the vast majority preferred a family over a career in the outside world, and most college men yearned for their own home. Another magazine even concluded that bachelors over the age of thirty must suffer from mental problems or else they would have been married by then. The magazine suggested that those malcontents seek psychiatric help.

The best step would be to have families conform to an ideal. Besides the vision of a two-parent home, the image of barbecues, a decent home, and clean-cut teenagers who frequented malt shops and obeyed parents, took hold. In 1953 the parents of one small Ohio town, to avoid grappling with the typical teenager response that "every other teenage does it," met and agreed on a list of rules, including nightly curfew and the age at which a girl could attend her first dance, that every family followed. Insurance statistics for these years showed that more than six hundred thousand men injured themselves each year, not in skiing accidents or mountain climbing, but with saws, hammers, and electrical tools during home repair projects.

The push to conformity extended into the educational realm. Local and state committees examined textbooks to see that they promoted patriotism and decency and to weed out anything they considered un-American. Teachers devised cautious lesson plans that avoided controversial topics out of fear that they might be fired for encouraging unpopular ideas. Two Houston, Texas, educators lost their jobs for reading from the works of D.H. Lawrence, a popular author who grappled with heated topics such as homosexuality. School boards could fire teachers simply for supporting a teacher union or for refusing to answer questions about their past or their political views. These actions discouraged free thinking and the critical examination of serious issues and produced a cadre of teachers and students who silently accepted the situation.

"In God We Trust"

Other factors besides family provide stability and comfort in times of stress. During the Korean War, many Americans turned to organized religion. Religion imparted order, discipline, and hope in a time when communism and the atom bomb offered insecurity and despair. Since religion offered a calm antidote to the turmoil produced by communism, the main threat to the nation's democratic manner of living, religious piety came to be associated strongly with patriotism. To be irreligious placed one among the ranks of godless Communists.

A few examples from these years show the importance religion had in American society. In 1952, a Supreme Court decision allowed public schools to grant release time to students specifically for religious instruction. Two years later Congress passed a law adding the words *under God* to the

During the Korean War, the American public emphasized the importance of a stable, two-parent home.

Pledge of Allegiance, and in 1956 the House of Representatives and the Senate in Washington, D.C., without a single dissenting vote, adopted a national motto, "In God We Trust."

Even President Eisenhower stepped into the religious picture. In 1954, to commem-

orate July 4, Eisenhower asked every American to spend time in prayer and penance. Many followed his suggestion, although the president, an ardent sportsman, still found time to fish in the morning, play eighteen holes of golf in the afternoon, and play cards that evening.

Politicians and educators were, of course, not the primary conveyors of religion at the time. The Reverend Billy Graham staged popular religious crusades around the United States, the Reverend Norman Vincent Peale penned a best-selling book, *The Power of Pos-* *itive Thinking,* and the Catholic bishop Fulton J. Sheen hosted a weekly television show that beamed into millions of homes. In response to this pervasive reach of religion, bookstores could hardly keep pace with the demand for the Bible; by 1953, they sold an amazing 10 million Bibles per year.

The Reverend Billy Graham addresses a massive crowd during his religious crusade across America.

Housing Boom

Another ingredient offering stability in an unstable age was the ability to own a home. World events might swirl out of control, but owning a home provided a touch of order in one's personal realm.

Sales of new houses slumped drastically in the 1930s because of the Great Depression; they continued to decline throughout World War II, when the war effort sapped most construction material. In the 1950s a rising birth rate, greater availability of material, and people eager to purchase homes kick-started a construction renaissance.

William J. Levitt, a construction company titan, stood at the forefront of the housing boom. He correctly understood that the greater numbers of automobiles on the roads, along with an improved highway system, would enable many Americans to leave the cluttered big-city apartment buildings and head to the country. He envisioned communities of affordable homes, much as Henry Ford had made it possible for Americans to purchase a car with the inexpensive Model T. Like Henry Ford, Levitt wanted his product available to the ordinary American, not merely the super-rich.

The secret lay in efficiency. Levitt took Ford's idea of mass production, in which each worker performed the same operation over and over, and adapted it to the housing market. He studied the building process and concluded that he could complete a home, from laying the foundation to installing a roof, in twenty-seven different steps. He then assembled twenty-seven teams of workers, each specializing in a single area. An individual team started at one house, completed its building task, then moved on to the next house, repeating the process throughout the planned community. Levitt's workers fine-tuned the process so efficiently that they could construct thirty-six houses every day.

Of course, the purchaser did not have many options. Henry Ford said that a customer could purchase his Model T Ford in any color he wanted, as long as the color was black, the only choice available. Levitt followed suit. The first Levitt homes, a community of seventeen thousand units built near Hempstead, Long Island, presented a prepackaged dwelling consisting of a living room, kitchen, two bedrooms, and a bathroom. He included a free Bendix washing machine and a new Admiral television set as an incentive to eager homebuyers. Workers planted new trees every twenty-eight feet. To further pare costs and lower the home's cost to below eight thousand dollars Levitt forewent adding a basement and opted for a cement slab foundation.

To make purchasing as simple as possible for the buyer, Levitt reduced the amount of paperwork to a minimum. He demanded no down payment or closing costs, and he took advantage of low-interest loans available to veterans.

Ownership Is Patriotism

Newspaper ads in March 1949 proclaimed, "You're a lucky fellow, Mr. Veteran. Uncle Sam and the world's largest builder have made it possible for you to live in a charming house in a delightful community without having to pay for them with your eye teeth."[57] One day after the ad appeared, a line of customers stretched out Levitt's office door to the street.

People rushed to Hempstead to purchase a house. They ignored the fact that each house basically offered the same floor plan and looked identical from outside. They wanted to own a home, and that was all that counted. Levitt enjoyed such phenomenal success that *Time* magazine placed him on its July 3, 1950, cover, standing in front of a row of identical Levitt houses, with the caption "For Sale: A New Way of Life."[58]

Everyone appeared to benefit. Levitt amassed a fortune, consumers gained an answer to their prayers, and, strangely enough, the nation acquired another weapon in the battle against communism. Levitt boasted not only of the quality and inexpensive price of his homes but also how ownership hampered the spread of communism. "No man who owns his own house and lot can be a Communist," he loved to state. Not only does the purchaser have too much at stake in the new product, but "he has too much to do."[59] Other constructors soon followed in Levitt's footsteps to erect communities of their own around the country.

Conformity, Not Communism

Living in one of the "Levittowns," as the public labeled them, offered benefits, but they contained drawbacks as well, for *Levittown* and *conformity* became synonymous. Regulations banned the addition of fences. Lawns had to be mowed at least once a week in season, and housewives could not hang wet clothes on the outside clothesline on weekends.

If anyone wanted diversity—and few did in the conformist home front of the Korean War—Levittown was not the answer, for most of the buyers came from the same class—young married couples between the ages of twenty-five and thirty-five. Few single parents or elderly dotted the list of inhabitants, and not a single African American was to be seen. People lived in Levittowns precisely for the conformity. Any obvious differences were discouraged or outlawed. As one observer wrote, "An otherwise minor variation becomes blatant deviance; a man who paints his garage fire-engine red in a block where the rest of the garages are white has literally and psychologically made himself a marked man."[60] People distrusted challenges to the status quo—the way things were—and rather than incur their neighbors' wrath, occupants simply went along with the tide.

Critics observed the housing phenomena created by Levitt and his competitors and decried the emphasis on conformity. They stated that it was almost as if society advocated a nation of robots, and they compared home dwellers to the sterile pod people from the movie *Invasion of the Body Snatchers*.

The influential social commentator Lewis Mumford had no use for Levittowns because

"That Suburban Dream Life"

The homes William J. Levitt constructed offered more than a shelter to most people. They delivered a new lifestyle, the answer to many people's dreams. By later standards the houses may have shrunk in both comparison and size, but for middle-class America in the 1950s, they stood as the ideal. In her 1993 oral history of the decade, *The Fifties: A Women's Oral History,* journalist Brett Harvey includes the following words of Cece Roberts, a woman who moved into a Levitt house.

> I was twenty-five and pregnant. We'd been living in a one-room apartment on the lower east side of Manhattan, and though I liked the city streets, the hurly-burly, I couldn't envision raising children there. I wanted that suburban dream life.
>
> The [Levitt] house was surrounded by a lake of mud. But I was thrilled—it was a very exciting thing to have a house of your own. And everything you dreamed about was there, everything was working, brand-new, no cockroaches.

Prepackaged Levitt homes line a street near Long Island, New York.

of this march to conformity. He wrote that the communities were no more than

> a multitude of uniform, unidentifiable houses, lined up inflexibly, at uniform distances on uniform roads, in a tree-

less command waste, inhabited by people of the same class, the same incomes, the same age group, witnessing the same television performances, eating the same tasteless prefabricated foods, from the same freezers, conforming in

every outward and inward respect to a common mold manufactured in the same central metropolis.[61]

An aerial view shows a suburban community of Levitt tract homes. Many considered Levittowns to be too uniform.

He decried the lack of diversity and individuality and believed that society would suffer as a result.

At the same time, the rush to the suburbs caused an accompanying decline in big northern cities, a trend that has yet to be reversed in some regions. The rise of suburbs left less time for some families to spend to-gether during the day since one member had to drive a distance to work. Likewise, the suburbs impeded the burgeoning drive for women's rights by isolating many females from the workplace and confining them in their suburban homes.

However, positive and negative effects come with any new development, and although Levittowns had their share of problems, they did offer many Americans their first opportunity to grasp that great American dream—home ownership. More than 1.5 million Americans took advantage and departed New York City alone for the suburbs during the fifties.

The American Dream Car

Another part of the American dream was to drive to and from that home in a brand new car, and the larger the automobile was, the better it was thought to be. People on the home front during the Korean War had more money, and car manufacturers made sure they offered tempting alternatives.

General Motors took the lead among automotive companies by establishing a practice that is now commonplace—introducing new car models every year. Keep the consumers hungry, was the attitude, and by churning out yearly models General Motors believed consumers would not long be satisfied with the car they already owned—they would always be comparing what they had to the newer, more advanced models.

Like much else on the home front, General Motors tried to place people into prearranged categories instead of focusing on individuality. They appealed to shared attitudes and values and created specific vehicles to market to these groups. General Motors saw in conformity a mass-marketing tool with which to entice the public and to amass fabulous profits.

General Motors produced the Chevrolet, the least expensive car made by the company, for young couples without much money and for blue-collar workers. The Pontiac was designed for people with a little more money, the Oldsmobile for the established businessman, and the Buick for doctors, lawyers, and young business executives.

At the top stood the Cadillac, the car that symbolized status, achievement, and success. If one could afford a Cadillac, then one had unquestioningly attained the American dream. Consumers zooming from home to work in their Chevrolets and Buicks might be content with that model, but they always had the Cadillac as the ultimate goal. Singer Elvis Presley purchased Cadillacs by the

Supplies for Levittown

The phenomenal success of the various Levittowns that dotted the nation had ripple effects that created other thriving concerns. Eugene Ferkauf saw his opportunity with the original Levitt homes near Hempstead, Long Island. He figured that such a conglomeration of homes formed a perfect market for all sorts of goods. Those empty dwellings needed appliances and tools, and the inhabitants would certainly require clothes. On December 2, 1953, Ferkauf opened his first store only ten minutes from Levittown. The superstore, the first of its type in the nation, contained different departments for consumer convenience. Ferkauf correctly predicted its success, and so many customers besieged his workers that Ferkauf had coffee and sandwiches brought in to the store so the sales people would not have to leave the floor. From that beginning, Ferkauf expanded his stores, which he called E.J. Korvettes.

handful for himself, his family, and friends, and other prominent individuals made that their first purchase after receiving a large promotion at work.

Roadside Innovations

Along with the increased purchase of automobiles came another adaptation during the Korean War that took advantage of the home front's penchant for uniformity. While on a vacation drive to Washington, D.C., with his family, businessman Kemmons Wilson became repeatedly frustrated at the inability to locate a clean, dependable motel or restaurant along America's highways. At the end of each day, weary after a long stretch of driving, he had to search through whatever town at which he arrived for something

decent enough for his family. He rarely discovered anything that suited his desires. Standards varied from location to location; Wilson never knew if he could expect quality service as he pulled into a motel parking lot.

Determined to rectify the situation, Wilson studied the rooms along his route, both good and bad, and drew up a list of what he thought consumers would want. He concluded that, above all, they wanted uniformity and familiarity, that a room and service in one state would be the same as in another.

When he returned from this vacation, he organized a business venture to construct hundreds of similar motels, each offering

Cadillacs like this one were the ultimate status symbol of the early 1950s.

The McDonald's drive-in was one of the earliest fast food restaurants in the United States.

the same product and each one located at major intersections along the highways so that drivers could easily find them. His motels contained clean rooms, a restaurant, a gift shop, and a swimming pool, and they offered television sets and air conditioning in every room. Wilson took every available step to guarantee that families out for an extended trip could count on a reliable motel offering similar amenities no matter where they traveled.

The first in his chain, which he named Holiday Inn after a popular movie starring Bing Crosby, opened in August 1952. Kemmons Wilson tapped a national need at the right time and took advantage of the national mood for uniformity to launch what became one of the most successful stories in the industry.

Fast Food

At the same time, other individuals were transforming the restaurant business. Like Wilson and General Motors, they relied on the desire for uniformity to build their product. In 1940, Dick and Maurice McDonald opened a drive-in restaurant in San Bernardino, California, that relied on speed of service and a simplified menu to service more customers. Patrons knew they would not have a multitude of choices from which to select, but that is not what they wanted anyway—they wanted decent food delivered quickly. McDonald's restaurants offered hamburgers, milk shakes, and french fries and promised to have customers in and out in no time.

"The Beauty in a Hamburger Bun"

Ray Kroc proved to be a visionary in the restaurant business who brought quality food at an affordable price to customers. The occupation was not simply a job to Kroc, however. He had a true love for his product and for serving it to his customers. He could even wax eloquent about something as simple as the hamburger bun. David Halberstam included the following Ray Kroc quote in his book *The Fifties:*

> Consider, for example, the hamburger bun. It requires a certain kind of mind to see the beauty in a hamburger bun. Yet is it any more unusual to find grace in the texture and softly curved silhouette of a bun than to reflect lovingly on the hackles of a favorite fishing fly? Or the arrangements and textures and colors in a butterfly's wings? Not if you're a McDonald's man. Not if you view the bun as an essential material in the art of serving a great many meals fast. Then this plump yeasty mass becomes an object worthy of sober study.

During the Korean War the McDonald brothers handed consumers in one location what they wanted—uniformity—but it was up to another man with a keen eye for the future, Ray Kroc, to take the concern nationwide. Like Kemmons Wilson, Kroc intended to place McDonald's drive-ins in every town and offer the same products at the same prices. He appealed to young families that wanted an inexpensive night out with their children, and he emphasized uniformity in food so that no matter where in the nation someone purchased a hamburger or french fries, they tasted the same.

Kroc succeeded because he strictly emphasized thrift and economy of practice. He standardized the McDonald's hamburger at 1.6 ounces of meat fashioned into a patty 3 and 5/8 inches in diameter. The fat content could not exceed 20 percent, and every hamburger came premade with a quarter-ounce of onion, a teaspoon of mustard, a tablespoon of ketchup, and one pickle one inch in diameter. Kroc became infamous in the company for suddenly showing up at a local McDonald's, carefully picking up unused packets of salt and ordering workers to scrape out every available amount of ketchup from the large containers.

Kroc epitomized the American way of life at a time when communism posed a serious challenge. He worked hard, but his labor was for an inner satisfaction rather than for material possessions. "I have never worshiped money and I have never worked for money," Kroc stated. "I worked for pride and accomplishment. Money can become a nuisance. It's a hell of a lot more fun chasin' it than gettin' it. The fun is in the race."[62]

Like much around him, he also viewed his work as a battle, a competition against other individuals who wanted nothing more than to triumph at his expense, just as communism hoped to win out over democracy. He was not about to let that happen. In words that were reminiscent of Mike Hammer and that just as easily could have been spoken about the struggle between the diverse styles of the United States and the Soviet Union, he claimed that the fast-food business was "rat eat rat, dog eat dog. I'll kill 'em [competitors] and I'm going to kill 'em before they kill me. You're talking about the American way of survival of the fittest." He also boasted of rivals that "if they were drowning to death I'd put the hose in their mouth."[63] Like soldiers battling communism in the field or federal investigators unearthing spies inside the nation, Kroc and McDonald's showed that the American way of commerce and competition enjoyed far more success than the Communist manner of production.

Although the American nation yearned for conformity and calmness at home during the Korean War, and in many instances obtained it, other events showed that uniformity and peace had yet to be obtained. This was especially true in the area of civil rights. While the armed forces struggled overseas to bring democracy to a foreign land, at home democracy was denied to American citizens.

Chapter 6

Full Democracy at Home

The country's desire for uniformity and normalcy camouflaged the fact that, besides the Communist threat, serious disorders existed within American society during the Korean War. In one way, however, the war actually helped one group of citizens to gain improved treatment. The most important social issue affected by the war concerned the unfair treatment extended to the nation's African Americans.

"The Law Has Made Him Equal"

Abuse of African Americans by white Americans dated back to the time of slavery. Even though the Civil War and civil rights amendments of the 1800s legally ended slavery, the laws could only state what was legal and illegal. It could not force people to accept others as equal. The noted defense attorney Clarence Darrow mentioned in a famous 1926 courtroom case involving prejudice that "the law has made him [the African American] equal, but man has not."[64]

Thus, many instances of bigotry flared on the home front during the Korean War. In the summer of 1951, Harvey E. Clark, an African American military veteran, attempted to move his family to a quiet apartment in Cicero, Illinois, an all-white suburb outside of Chicago. Clark encountered bitter opposition, including a warning from the chief of police to leave "or you'll get a bullet through you."[65] When that failed to deter Clark, an angry mob of four thousand whites, free to act since both Cicero's mayor and the chief of police were conveniently out of town, damaged his apartment building and ruined most of his belongings.

The state militia eventually had to be called in to restore order. A grand jury later charged seven Cicero police officers with violating the Clarks' civil rights. Four of the officers were found guilty, and the National Association for the Advancement of Colored People (NAACP) organized fund-raisers to help replace the Clarks' destroyed belongings.

As this incident showed, resistance to integration took place in the North as well as in the South, where, for instance, African American activists in Mississippi sometimes found their names and deeds printed in newspapers and their jobs no longer waiting for them. Even Levittown, that successful builder of the American dream for so many, closed its doors to African Americans. In an interview, William Levitt explained why he did not sell to blacks. His attitude reflected that of millions of Americans throughout the nation in the 1950s:

Harvey E. Clark and his wife were forced from their Chicago home by an angry mob of whites.

As a Jew I have no room in my mind or heart for racial prejudice. But I have come to know that if we sell one house to a Negro family, then 90 or 95 percent of our white customers will not buy into the community. As a company our position is simply this: We can solve a housing problem, or we can try to solve a racial problem but we cannot combine the two.[66]

Conditions in the States

Conditions for African Americans had only marginally improved since the nation first entered the twentieth century. Near the end of World War II, the popular radio commentator Walter Winchell asked an African American woman what punishment German leader Adolf Hitler deserved. Without hesitation the woman thought of the appropriate retribution for someone who started a war that killed millions of people and produced the Holocaust. "Paint him black and send him over here,"[67] replied the woman, only half joking.

When African Americans campaigned for better treatment, some citizens countered that if they thought life in the United States was so bad, they should leave and move to the Soviet Union. Few took up the offer, but the attitude showed that many white Americans were content to leave conditions as they were. They wanted normalcy and uniformity, not chaos and strife. Civil rights activism had little place in their image of what they expected in the post–World War II United States.

The U.S. government outwardly condemned racism, of course. It could not approve of actions that violated the law or denied an individual his or her civil rights, especially when the Soviet Union included every instance of bigotry in America in its propaganda as proof of democracy's failure. The U.S. government had to appear to the world to be supporting equal rights as a step in showcasing democracy over communism.

A Plea for Equality

The portion of government that most assisted civil rights during the Korean War turned out to be the military. Blacks first made headway in integrating combat units. After conditions changed in the military, those same changes later became easier to implement throughout the rest of society.

During World War II blacks could only serve in segregated units. After the war a group of African American leaders approached President Truman and emphasized that African Americans would not much longer be willing to "shoulder a gun and fight for democracy abroad unless full democracy was obtained at home."[68] The power and logic of their argument was not lost on Truman. On July 26, 1948, he issued Executive Order 9981, which called for the complete integration of the armed forces.

Announcing an order is one thing, enforcing it is another. Thurgood Marshall, a prominent black lawyer for the NAACP, studied integration in the military and found that although more African Ameri-

An all-black infantry unit in Korea advances to the front lines of battle.

cans had entered one of the services, treatment had not improved. He examined the results of courts-martial, for instance, and discovered that black soldiers were convicted at a far higher rate than white soldiers who committed comparable crimes.

By the time war erupted in Korea, integration had not yet been implemented in the army. Black and white soldiers served in their own units because the army feared the effects of mixing races. Consigned to their own companies and battalions, African American soldiers had little reason to train or perform well. After all, the army chain of command considered them to be inferior.

The performance of African American units in early combat was thus hardly surprising. The all-black Twenty-fourth Infantry Regiment, one of three regiments composing the Twenty-fifth Infantry Division (the other regiments were all-white units), gained

"You're Always Going to Be out of Step"

Any member of a minority group who lived in the United States during the Korean War knows that African Americans were not the only people to battle discrimination. Females who vied for leadership positions in business, no matter what race, encountered resistance from many segments of society. Journalist Brett Harvey includes the following quote of Ellen Rodgers, a female who entered the typically all-male domain of engineering, in her 1993 oral history of the decade, *The Fifties: A Women's Oral History.*

I don't think the ladies in the town accepted the fact that I worked. That was the point at which I said to myself, "Well, you're always going to be out of step and you might as well face it."

Every time I'd have to call vendors, for example, to get information about their products, I would have to start very aggressively right at the beginning by stating that I was an *engineer* with this firm and I needed information. Because otherwise I invariably got fobbed off [ignored] because they assumed I was a secretary, or a housewife wanting information on some product.

a speedy reputation for "bugging out," a slang term for leaving the scene of fighting. During one skirmish most of one company rushed from the battlefield, leaving their white commanding officer and a few riflemen to fend off the enemy.

White units also performed poorly in the initial stages of Korean combat, but the Twenty-fourth faced a unique situation. Replacements for inadequate soldiers could be quickly shuttled in for the white regiments, but due to a dearth of black infantrymen and officers, few of the incompetents could be removed. The Twenty-fourth had to fight with the original group of men, but white units had the luxury of learning which men it could not count on, then sending them to the rear.

"High Time We Stopped This Business"

Treatment back home failed to improve, either. The incident involving Sergeant John Rice, although not an African American, indicates the extent of the double standard toward whites and nonwhites. A Winnebago Indian, Rice had been slain in combat. The army shipped his body home to Sioux City, Iowa, for burial, where family members and other mourners gathered at the local cemetery. As they prepared to begin the service, cemetery officials stepped in and refused to allow it because Rice was not a Caucasian. Sadly, the family had to return Rice's body to the funeral home and make other arrangements.

Fortunately, the next day President Truman read of the incident in the newspapers. He exploded in anger at the inequity, then issued an invitation to Mrs. Rice to bury her husband in Arlington National Cemetery in Washington, D.C. Truman also ordered that a government airplane pick up the body and family and transport them to the capital.

The North Koreans and the Soviet Union took advantage of this and other instances of unfair treatment toward minorities to advocate their Communist systems of government. They mocked the United States for boasting about being the world's foremost democracy while extending shabby treatment toward its own citizens. A North Korean propaganda pamphlet, in an effort to gain advocates among America's African American community, stated, "Today, under the orders of a Southern U.S. President (President Truman came from Missouri), U.S. planes are bombing and strafing COLORED PEOPLE in Korea."[69]

Some newspapers realized the predicament Truman faced and urged more movement toward equality. In Ohio, the *Cleveland Plain Dealer* praised him after the John Rice incident and stated in an editorial that "it is high time we stopped this business. We can't do it as decent human beings and we can't do it as a nation trying to sell democracy to a world full of non-white peoples."[70]

"Misery Loves Company"

Other forms of the national media exerted pressure on the government to guarantee the civil rights of the country's African

Thurgood Marshall (fourth from left) poses with fellow members of the NAACP legal team.

Americans. Television, so prominent in the rise and fall of Senator Joseph McCarthy, aired documentaries on race relations, and newspapers and magazines assigned reporters full time to cover the movement. As individuals in the United States saw instances of bigotry being highlighted by the media, they became more educated about the issue, and a growing number were outraged over the injustice.

During the Korean War, though, the most potent factor advancing the cause of equality proved to be the military. The armed forces did not take the appropriate steps because they felt a sense of duty to the nation's minorities. Some top-ranking officers undoubtedly advocated better treatment, but the drive to complete integration within the military arose out of practicality—it made more sense and gave greater efficiency to the services.

First of all, the U.S. Army simply needed more men fighting in Korea, especially when North Korean and Chinese forces practically shoved the United States off the peninsula. Many all-white units, besieged by the enemy, suffered enormous casualties. Undermanned and ill suited to stop the Communists, the U.S. military in Korea faced total disaster unless some remedy became immediately apparent.

The military turned to African American soldiers, serving behind the lines in Korea as support troops, to fill the depleted ranks. Faced with the choice of fighting at a great disadvantage or leveling the odds by rushing African American troops to the front, officers had few objections to commanding mixed units. Colonel John G. Hill, who saw intense combat, explained, "We would have been doing ourselves a disservice to permit [African American] soldiers to lie around in rear areas at the expense of the still further weakening of our [white] rifle companies."[71]

A white soldier of the Ninth Infantry Regiment typified the reaction of most men. He said most everyone welcomed the arrival of the African American troops "because at a time like that [fighting with their backs to the wall], misery loves company."[72] Platoon leader Herbert M. Hart claimed that in the bloody combat, most soldiers quickly overcame any objections to fighting side by side with an African American. He mentioned that "it didn't make any difference if you are white, red, black, green, or turquoise to the men over there."[73]

Performance Improves

Once the African American soldiers entered the front lines and contributed to the fighting, white soldiers absorbed a different impression of their abilities. When given the opportunity to enter combat in integrated units, black soldiers fought as well as whites. As many African Americans volunteered for dangerous missions as white soldiers. When confined to segregated platoons and companies, which imparted the notion that the black soldiers were not as talented or as brave as white soldiers, African Americans performed more poorly. Now, having the opportunity to fight as an equal alongside

A racially mixed unit in Korea poses for a portrait. Most white soldiers in Korea welcomed the arrival of African American troops.

their white cohorts, morale and performance among the African Americans improved.

Factors behind the lines also fueled the drive for equality. The army custom in training camps had always been to train whites and blacks separately. With Korean battlefield commanders begging for fresh troops, however, officers in stateside facilities felt an urgent need to streamline the training process and get those soldiers over to Korea more quickly. An obvious solution was to place recruits in their units in the order in which they entered camp, regardless of color, instead of waiting for enough white or black soldiers to form a new company.

Some officers, comfortable with the old style of doing things, predicted dire out-

comes from integration, but once they saw the results, their doubts largely dissolved. Most of the soldiers, black and white, quickly adapted to the situation.

Brigadier General Frank McConnell, commander at one of the training facilities, said, "I would see recruits, Negro and white, walking down the street off-duty, all grouped together. The attitude of the Southern soldiers was that this was the army way; they accepted it the same way they accepted getting up at 5:30 in the morning."[74]

Officers and soldiers ignored the negative assumptions about racial differences that kept bigotry alive and allowed the new system to work. McConnell and others like him went ahead and did what needed doing, and in the long run they proved the fallacy of those assumptions.

The Military Assists Integration

In integrated units, African American soldiers repeatedly proved their worth under fire. Hundreds of black officers held command positions, and Captain Daniel "Chappie" James Jr. flew 101 combat missions, earning a Distinguished Flying Cross in the process. More than five thousand African Americans died in combat.

Two who perished earned the country's highest award for valor, the Medal of Honor. The military issued the war's first Medal of Honor to Private First Class William Thompson, who, in August 1950, while the remainder of his company fled in panic, calmly remained with his machine gun and fired at the onrushing North Korean troops until he was killed. Sergeant Cornelius H. Charlton was awarded the same medal in June 1951. Despite suffering from wounds that eventually caused his death, Charlton led three attacks against North Korean forces along a ridge and drove them off before he died.

Between the months of May and August 1951, the number of soldiers serving in integrated units rose from 9 percent to 30 percent. By 1954, the army had completed the process of integrating every unit. Its success inspired similar programs in the other branches of the military, and before long the navy, marines, and air force joined the army in having total integration.

The effective integration of the armed forces had repercussions on the home front as well. Hundreds of white soldiers returned home with an improved attitude toward African Americans. After all, they had stood side by side and battled the enemy, and many white soldiers had witnessed black soldiers die for their nation. That could not help but alter impressions formed from ignorance and bias. When these men headed home from Korea, they brought those impressions with them.

The military also affected the areas surrounding military bases inside the United States. African American soldiers, even in bases inside the Deep South, freely walked into clubs and cafés catering to the military. Should any serious opposition arise, most officers tried to take steps to prevent further occurrences. For instance, when one bar owner near a camp located in the North refused to serve black soldiers, an officer threatened to declare the bar off-limits to all soldiers unless the owner quickly complied and permitted African American soldiers in his establishment. Faced with a disastrous loss of income, the bar owner opened his doors.

"Slowly Stealing a Teaspoonful of Your Self-Esteem"

While the military integrated its forces, events on the home front also prodded the nation toward granting full equality to all of its citizens. Progress in racial relations in the United States moved slowly, but it did take a few giant steps that later led to even more effective measures.

When the United States entered the Korean War, the nation had two public school systems, one for white students and the other for black students. The nation justified the dual school systems because of a Supreme Court ruling of 1896 that stated, in part, that separate schools could be set up for whites and blacks as long as they provided equal services to both races.

A surface glance might convey the notion that separate schools, as long as they offered the same benefits, caused no harm. That assumption suffers in many ways.

A teacher instructs a class of African American children at a segregated school. The U.S. Supreme Court banned separate educational facilities in 1954.

Black southern schools never received the same material or financial support as their white counterparts. Even if they did, the most insidious aspect of segregation was neither money, textbooks, nor classrooms but rather the harm it inflicted to the spirit of the children who were, in effect, told they were different and not as important as the white boys and girls who attended the better schools.

Melba Patillo Beals, who later in the decade helped integrate the Little Rock, Arkansas, public school system by being one of nine African American students to attend the city's previously all-white high school, wrote in her memoir,

> Black folks aren't born expecting segregation, prepared from day one to follow its confining rules. Nobody presents you with a handbook when you're teething and says, "Here's how you must behave as a second-class citizen." Instead, the humiliating expectations and traditions of segregation creep over you, slowly stealing a teaspoonful of your self-esteem each day.[75]

In the early 1950s, African American leaders intended to challenge the separate-but-equal doctrine. Led by Thurgood Marshall and the NAACP, they claimed that separate schools were, by nature, unequal, and therefore illegal. They argued that southern states spent twice as much money on white schools and four times as much for building maintenance. White teachers earned 30 per-

NAACP lawyer Thurgood Marshall argued that segregated schools were unequal and illegal.

cent more in salary than African American educators, and few, if any, buses were available to transport black students to their schools.

Brown v. Board of Education

In 1951, Oliver Brown, an African American parent from Kansas, angered that his daughter had to walk twenty-one blocks to reach her all-black school each day when a white public school stood only seven blocks from her home, filed suit in court against the Topeka, Kansas, Board of Education to change the law. With the assistance of the NAACP, the case worked its way to the Supreme Court, where the justices engaged in heated debate over the legality of separate-but-equal institutions.

Although the public remained divided on the issue, many people had come to the conclusion that the United States had to practice what it preached and grant equality to all citizens. Otherwise, how could Americans turn to other nations in the world, especially the Communist countries, and proclaim to be the model of enlightened living? The nation sent young men into battle in Korea to safeguard democracy yet simultaneously denied full benefits to people on the home front. Some believed that if the system of democracy established in the United States was to prevail over communism, then democracy must be open to everyone. The attorney general of the United States reflected that attitude when he stated that "racial discrimination furnishes grist for the Communist propaganda mills, and it raises doubt even among friendly nations as to the intensity of our devotion to the democratic faith."[76]

Fortunately for the nation, Earl Warren headed the Supreme Court. The farsighted individual understood that, unless the Court could convince the country of the rightness, not simply the legality, of eliminating separate-but-equal institutions, its decision would be greeted with skepticism. To that end he set out to persuade his eight cohorts on the Supreme Court to vote in favor of Oliver Brown, even though some

Earl Warren

The Supreme Court chief justice who orchestrated the unanimous vote in the *Brown v. Board of Education* decision, one of the most momentous rulings in civil rights history, had a spotty record in civil rights before joining the Supreme Court. Born in Los Angeles, he served three terms as the state governor from 1943 through 1952. He shot to national fame immediately after the Japanese attack on Pearl Harbor brought war to the United States. California contained a large Japanese American population, a fact that worried politicians, the military, and civilians alike. Could this population be a safe nest for Japanese ready to sabotage American industries or military installations?

With the consent of the federal government, Earl Warren enacted what is now considered one of the most sweeping assaults on civil liberties by ordering the state's Japanese American citizens confined to relocation centers. Japanese businessmen had to close their businesses, and families had to leave their houses. In the emotional aftermath of Pearl Harbor, however, Warren's actions were not viewed as harsh measures.

In 1953 President Dwight D. Eisenhower selected him chief justice of the Supreme Court. Once on the Court, Warren turned his talents to ensuring rights for individuals. Among them was a case from Kansas that helped bring down the bitter walls of segregation.

"The American Negro Needs a Gandhi"

The national media descended on Mississippi to cover the trial of the men accused in the murder of Emmett Till. One of those who wrote about the trial, I.F. Stone, delivered a harsh message to the nation, a country he considered stuck in the throes of bigotry. In his October 3, 1955, column, which was reprinted in his 1963 book *The Haunted Fifties,* he called the verdict of not guilty against the accused "a verdict of guilty against all the rest of us and our country.... To the outside world it must look as if the conscience of white America has been silenced, and the appearance is not too deceiving."

Stone commented on the suggestion that African Americans march on Washington, D.C., to protest the verdict. His words form a connection between the Till case and the birth of the modern civil rights movement:

> The American Negro needs a Gandhi to lead him, and we need the American Negro to lead us. If he does not provide leadership against the sickness in the South, the time will come when we will all pay a terrible price for allowing a psychopathic racist brutality to flourish unchecked.

Not long after the Till murder Martin Luther King Jr., a devotee of Gandhi, rose to prominence and guided the civil rights movement to new heights.

justices came from southern states where separate-but-equal policies were a way of life.

Through tireless effort, Warren finally achieved a unanimous vote, and on May 17, 1954, the Supreme Court issued one of the most famous proclamations in the history of the country. In *Brown v. Board of Education* the justices declared that "separate educational facilities are inherently unequal" and added that students forced to attend such institutions have been "deprived of the equal protection of the laws"[77] as stated in the Constitution. With this momentous announcement, the Supreme Court legally ended segregation.

A mixed reaction greeted the decision. The governors of Mississippi, Georgia, and South Carolina threatened to abolish all public schools rather than permit the integration of black and white students. Fiery crosses, the infamous symbol of the white supremacist organization the Ku Klux Klan, lit the skies

in certain cities, and on her way home from school after the decision had been announced, Melba Patillo Beals was attacked by an angry white man.

Numerous people in the nation, who yearned for conformity and uniformity and were thus rattled by the disturbing events in civil rights, nevertheless agreed with the sentiments expressed by the *Knoxville Journal.* The influential Tennessee newspaper, whose readership included many who protested the Supreme Court decision, stated, "No citizen, fitted by character and intelligence to sit as a justice of the Supreme Court, and sworn to uphold the Constitution of the United States, could have decided this question other than the way it was decided."[78]

On Toward the Civil Rights Movement

The events that took place on the home front during the Korean War prodded African

Americans to a more active role in civil rights. The number of African American leaders stepping up to take a more aggressive stance toward equality rose to the point where they were willing to contest actions that violated their fundamental rights. They believed that to do otherwise would have demeaned the sacrifice of those African American soldiers who fought, and died, in the Korean War.

This more activist attitude appeared in 1955, following the brutal death of young Emmett Till. In August the fourteen-year-old African American from Chicago, Illinois, visited relatives living in Mississippi. Unaccustomed with the local customs, which still relegated African Americans to a subservient role, Till offended a white woman by speaking to her. On August 24 the woman's husband and brother dragged Till from his relatives' house, severely beat the youth, shot him, attached a huge factory fan to the body as a weight, and dumped Till's body in the Tallahatchie River.

When news of the brutal incident spread across the country, African American leaders vowed to seek justice. The two men stood trial on murder charges, which took place in a courtroom packed with white supporters. After deliberating for barely more than one hour the jury—one of whom joked the verdict would have arrived sooner had they all not stopped to have soda—acquitted the men.

Though the accused were found not guilty (the pair later admitted their guilt to a reporter for a national magazine), the Till case continued the momentum toward equality created during the Korean War. One hundred days after Till's murder, Rosa Parks refused to leave her seat on a Montgomery, Alabama, bus. Shortly after that, a young minister came to her defense. Martin Luther King Jr. used the Rosa Parks incident as a launching spot for the civil rights movement he so ably led over the next decade.

Chapter 7

Youth Rebellion

As if turmoil over the Communist threat, both at home and abroad, was not enough to disrupt American society, another factor arose during the early 1950s that added further mayhem—rebelliousness, particularly among the nation's youth, against the norm. Whereas most adults hoped that conformity could lend a calming influence over events, the younger generation turned to new ideas, new music, and new attitudes. This division surfaced during the Korean War and laid the foundation for the more violent strife that rent American society during the late 1950s and into the 1960s.

"Why Did You Leave Me?"

Rebelliousness versus acceptance, individuality versus conformity—almost every American teenager struggled with these opposites, even if they did not understand them. Rod Serling, the gifted writer of numerous television and movie scripts of the 1950s and 1960s, wrote, "There was a postwar mystifi-

cation of the young, a gradual erosion of confidence in their elders, in the so-called truths, in the whole litany of moral codes."[79]

Television shows and magazines might picture the United States as wholesome and stable, but once beyond those narrow confines, an examination of society showed that the home front during the Korean War was fraught with crevices. Instances of juvenile delinquency so frequently appeared in the news that the *Saturday Evening Post* labeled it "the Shame of America,"[80] and younger people questioned their parents' motives.

One magazine article directed toward parents warned,

> Listen you—do you *really* think your kids are like bobby soxers in those wholesome Coca-Cola ads? Don't you know that across the table from you at dinner sits somebody who looks on you as an enemy who is planning to kill him in the immediate future? Don't you know that if you were to say to your Eng-

lish class, "It is raining," they would take it for granted you were a liar? Don't you know they never tell you nothing? That they can't? That they simply can't get through, can't, and won't even try anymore to communicate. Don't you know this, really? If you don't, you're heading for a terrible awakening.[81]

Younger people doubted the rightness of society and questioned the family unit. They wondered if the adult generation had abandoned them by not trying

Actor James Dean (seated on motorcycle) projected a rebellious image that appealed to much of America's youth.

to empathize with them. That is one reason why Marlon Brando, James Dean, Elvis Presley, and other teen idols gained such immense adulation in the 1950s. Besides their immense talents, these youth icons seemed to covet a rebel image, an image whose appeal was not understood by adults.

Actor James Dean said as much about his troubled life, which included the death of his mother when Dean was young and his father's abandoning him shortly thereafter. Another actor asked him what factors contributed to the burning intensity with which he performed, and Dean, who was reared by an aunt and uncle, replied it was anger toward his parents:

> Because I hate my mother and father. I wanted to get up onstage and I wanted to show them [I could be something]. I'll tell you what made me want to become an actor, what gave me the drive to want to be the best. My mother died when I was almost nine. I used to sneak out of my uncle's house and go to her grave, and I used to cry and cry on her grave—Mother, why did you leave me? I need you . . . I want you.[82]

Thus, the nation's youth held aloft the rebel image, even if they had no idea what they might want in place of their parents' world. "They protest segregation and [bomb] testing and the hollowness of their parents," wrote one critic in an article about the young, "but they cannot yet say what they are for, what new society they desire. They are only *against,* but that at least is a beginning."[83]

Rock and Roll Arrives

On a grand scale, the government battled communism overseas and at home, while on a smaller platform, many parents struggled to recapture a sense of calmness and stability out of the chaos generated by domestic problems and world events. All they had to do to confirm their suspicions that all was not well was to look at the music that emerged in the home front during the Korean War.

The new style of music originated as part of radio's response to its freshest competitor, television. In order to salvage its dwindling audience and to recapture those people who had switched to television, radio producers had to create a new product with which to lure an audience. Radio stations in northern cities had already begun to offer rhythm-and-blues music, a favorite of African American audiences, since so many African Americans had moved from the South to the large northern urban areas.

The music revolution that swept the nation's teens and frightened a generation of parents started with a Cleveland, Ohio, disc jockey named Alan Freed. Freed observed a new phenomenon—white teenagers purchasing rhythm-and-blues music. Figuring that he could fashion a successful radio show by playing that type of music, in 1951 Freed began playing rhythm-and-blues music on his late-night program. Since rhythm

Disk jockey Alan Freed poses with the group Lillian Leach and The Mellows. Freed coined the phrase "rock and roll."

and blues was associated with black audiences, and Freed wanted to appeal to the large white bloc, he changed the name of the music to rock and roll.

Freed's program rocketed in the ratings and launched a new era in the music industry. Instead of offering mainstream music that focused on uncontroversial subjects, rock and roll borrowed rhythm-and-blues slang that often dealt with taboo subjects, such as sex and drugs. Louder songs containing wilder outbursts marked the music, which at the same time enticed teenagers and repulsed adults.

In 1954, Bill Haley became the first huge sensation when he offered a wild version of the song "Shake, Rattle, and Roll." Haley's louder, more energetic style and pounding beat caught on with teenagers who were bored with their parents' more sedate tastes.

Haley, however, was a mere foreshadow of what was about to hit the nation. Another figure followed who paved the way for the rock explosion of the late 1950s and 1960s.

"Ah Just Act the Way Ah Feel"

A dynamic, handsome singer from Memphis, Tennessee, hoisted rock and roll to the top of the music industry. Born to a poor family in January 1935 in Tupelo, Mississippi, as a youth Elvis Presley enjoyed singing with church choirs, where he gained an appreciation for African American religious songs. As a unique gift for his mother's birthday in 1953, Presley made

Elvis Presley scandalized American parents with his sensual movements on stage.

a private recording at the Memphis Sound Studio (the family had moved to Memphis, Tennessee, in 1948), where he came to the notice of Sam Phillips, who owned Sun Records. Phillips had been searching for a white singer who captured the sound of black rhythm and blues, and with Presley he thought he had discovered the perfect mix.

Within a year Phillips released Presley's first single, "That's All Right, Mama," a combination of rhythm-and-blues and country-and-western music. At local concerts, crowds reacted with enthusiasm to Presley's flamboyant clothes, his hard-driving, soulful music, and his wild movements on stage. For the first time the audience, consisting mainly of younger Americans, witnessed searing emotion from a singer who belted out lines about passion and romance. A critic stated that the music scene had changed with Elvis Presley, whose performances made it clear that "there was no more pretense about moonlight and hand-holding; it was hard physical fact."[84]

Presley embarked upon his path to stardom during the Korean War, then soared to the top in the years following. In front of audiences packed with screaming teenage girls, Presley danced and sang his way to popularity. Almost single-handedly, in the first part of the 1950s Presley kicked off a process that eventually revolutionized the recording industry, in the process terrorizing millions of parents who feared the music corrupted their sons and daughters. Presley hardly fit their image of a wholesome individual who conformed; he even de-

scribed his sensual movements around stage as "Ah just act the way Ah feel."[85]

Parents did not want their daughters dating, or in this case listening to, someone who acted the way they felt. Uniformity, not individualism, was the desired norm in their opinion. As *Life* magazine concluded in surveying the scene, "Some American parents, without quite knowing what it is their kids are up to, are worried that it's something they shouldn't be."[86]

An article in *Look* magazine, one of the most popular of its day, in a forerunner of many such articles that would appear in magazines after the war, stated, "Presley is mostly nightmare,"[87] a performer who appealed mainly to the country's youth while throwing the adult world into a frenzy. In more conservative towns, radio stations fired disc jockeys who played Presley's records. One Chicago station smashed his records on the air, and a Cincinnati, Ohio, used-car dealer, to stir up sales, promised to smash fifty Elvis Presley records for each customer who visited the car lot. The New Haven, Connecticut, chief of police banned rock-and-roll parties.

Most people in the older generation, the men and women who suffered through World War II, sacrificed to purchase a home, and struggled to establish a stable manner of life only to see communism rise as a new threat, adhered to this alarming view. Rock and roll, Elvis Presley, and all the other pastimes that appealed to their children clashed with the world they wanted to strengthen and preserve.

The 1952 book *U.S.A. Confidential* expressed the feelings toward rock and roll:

Like a heathen religion, it is all tied up with tom-toms and hot jive and ritualistic orgies or erotic dancing, weed-smoking and mass mania, with African jungle background. Another cog in the giant delinquency machine is the radio disc jockey. We know that many platter-spinners are hopheads. Many others are Reds [Communists], left-wingers, or hecklers of social convention.[88]

The rock revolution disconcerted many parents during the Korean War, but they would eventually learn that this was only a foreshadow of things to come. Within a few years rock and roll, fueled by the examples of Alan Freed, Bill Haley, Elvis Presley, and others, would mount a more aggressive assault on society's foundations.

The "Beat" Culture

A corresponding attack on conformity that paralleled the youth movement also emerged from the adult world. Though smaller in scale and confined in location largely to a few big cities, the impact outgrew its numbers because of the literature left behind.

The "Beat" culture, or beatniks, as they were called, flourished in the Greenwich Village section of New York City and in San Francisco, California. Consisting of authors and poets who read their works at local coffeehouses, beatniks attacked the conformity that afflicted the nation in the wake of the Communist threat. Writers such as Allen Ginsberg and Jack Kerouac wrote vaguely of change and criticized what they called society's love of money and material comforts. They tried to define a new system in which they could believe, yet they had difficulty expressing much more than outrage over existing conditions.

Representative of this expression is J.D. Salinger's *Catcher in the Rye,* published in 1951. The main character, a youth named Holden Caulfield, struggles to find out who he is and what his role might be in what he considers a hypocritical world that plays according to a set of unwritten rules. The novel

The Beatniks

Several explanations exist for the origin of the word *beatnik.* One, stating that beatniks had been blessed with unusual insight into society, claims it was a shortened version of *beatitude,* a word referring to the sayings of Jesus Christ in his famous Sermon on the Mount. Another version takes an opposite stance: The word meant that the devotees were disillusioned with American society; in other words, they were "beaten down."

The movement started in California, then spread to the East Coast. Most people in the nation misunderstood them to be disciples of revolution, but they were far from it. Beatniks simply longed for peace and calm in their lives and the opportunity to express in writing their theories on modern society. According to a quote mentioned in Time-Life's *This Fabulous Century: 1950–1960,* author Jack Kerouac, one of the leading members of the beatniks, wrote, "We love everything—Bill Graham, the Big Ten, Rock and Roll, Zen, apple pie, Eisenhower—we dig it all. We're in the vanguard of the new religion."

soared to the best-seller lists and developed a cult following that persisted far beyond the 1950s.

"I Don't Get You"

As it did with the Communist menace, Hollywood produced films that examined youthful rebellion. Three movies garnered most of the attention and created further controversy between adults and teenagers.

In one of the early roles that shot Marlon Brando to prominence, 1954's *The Wild One* portrayed Brando as the tough leader of a motorcycle gang. The film deftly illustrated the mistrust that both the teen and the adult world had for each other.

As Johnny, the hard-edged leader of the Black Rebel motorcycle gang, Brando epitomizes the type many adults most fear—the antiestablishment youth who, while ranting against society, has nothing better to offer in its place. Loosely based on a true story, the tale takes two rival gangs into a typical American small town, where simply their presence terrorizes the inhabitants.

Violence, during which one person is killed, flares between the two gangs, leading the sheriff to order Brando and the others out of town. Before they drive away, the sheriff, representative of the adult world, tells Brando, who symbolizes the rebelliousness of youth, "I don't get you. I don't get your act at all, and I don't think you do either. I don't think you know what you're trying to do or how to go about it."[89]

Brando's most famous line from the film indicates the same. When a girl asks

American actor Marlon Brando starred in movies that examined youthful rebellion.

him what he is rebelling against, Brando sneers and asks, "What've you got?" Though the film's violence caused Great Britain to ban the movie, this role turned Brando into a major star, especially among younger viewers, and showed the split that cut across the nation's generations.

Rebel Without a Cause thrust James Dean, the ultimate 1950s rebel image, onto the big screen. Dean made only three films in a brief career that was cut short by his untimely September 1955 death in an automobile accident, but his sultry, haunting portrayals of troubled young men searching for happiness were images that struck home to many teens and created a large, devoted following of fans.

Long after his death, Dean remained the model of the disturbed, restless 1950s youth that he crafted in movies like *Rebel Without a Cause.* In that film, Dean's character attempts to make sense out of his world and determine his place in it, experiences through which almost every teenager passes. Adults try to offer simplistic solutions, such as go to school and follow the rules, while youths seek more complex answers.

The third film created a sensation for its graphic presentation of violence and chaos in the nation's public schools. In 1955 *Blackboard Jungle* took audiences into a big-city high school, where teachers grappled with juvenile delinquents for control of the institution. An energetic rock-and-roll sound track, highlighted by Bill Haley's "Rock Around the Clock," captivated younger audiences while repelling more conservative groups, who further associated rock and roll with juvenile delinquency and rebelliousness. Powerful performances by Glenn Ford as a teacher and Vic Morrow as the school "tough guy" attracted large audiences, but the film's violence and its depiction of juvenile delinquency caused many shocked parents to forbid their teenage sons and daughters from viewing it.

"All the Standards Are Harum-Scarum"

Reality was much more difficult to control than many thought. During the Korean War the nation's youth, who seemed ready to challenge older methods, collided with their parents' expectations for a calm, happy existence. This friction charted a course for more arduous years later for the different generations.

Nothing seemed to be the same anymore. An influential writer, Mark Sullivan, commented that "all the standards are harum-scarum. Children running the homes or the President of the United States barnstorming [campaigning] up and down the country—it's all the same dissolution of traditional, dependable ways."[90]

A current newspaper editor stated in an editorial that people wondered what was wrong with the nation. They looked about them and saw challenges to the system, and what made it more frustrating was that no one seemed to know what to do about it. In many ways, the world had moved on from what people imagined after World War II, and the thought frightened them. John Thornton of the navy mentioned of his return from the war, "We went away to Glenn Miller [a famous band leader of the 1940s who helped popularize swing music]. We came back to Elvis Presley."[91]

Dwight D. Eisenhower's election in 1952 appeared to stabilize conditions, for many Americans considered him to be a reminder of simpler times. As the top military commander in Europe during World War II, he personified the struggle against Adolf Hitler—Eisenhower stood for decency and goodness versus Hitler's evil. Possibly that symbol of goodness, who had admirably succeeded against Nazi Germany, could now halt the changes that afflicted American society.

A Perfect World

If Eisenhower could not, maybe television could. Of all the forms existing in the media, during the Korean War television most promoted the sense of family and conformity that many in the nation wanted. The industry rode a wave of popularity unequaled by anything since the heady days of radio in the 1930s and 1940s. Whereas in 1948 only 148,000 television sets existed

in the United States, within two years over 2 million households owned one. Consumers purchased televisions at the rate of 20,000 a day. In 1952 the initial issue of *TV Guide* hit the newsstands, and two years later the first TV dinners appeared in stores. By decade's end, an incredible 50 million television sets flooded the market.

Much of the programming mirrored the home front's desire for stability and uniformity. Few groundbreaking shows appeared on the weekly schedule, which was dominated by children's shows, news documentaries, and comedies dealing with the so-called "typical" American family. Like their cohorts in Hollywood, few television producers intended to risk their careers by offering controversial topics that might gain the ire of men like Senator Joseph McCarthy.

Two television series illustrate the point. Each captured a large share of the market and created an enthusiastic following, but

A Youthful Chatter

Many of the nation's parents had difficulty adjusting to their teens' customs because so much appeared alien to what they had experienced. They hoped the newer generation would turn out the same as theirs had, but when younger people rebelled in different ways, parents became alarmed. One indication appeared in the newer language with which the teens communicated. They had their own forms of communication, none of which easily blended with that of their parents.

In the Time-Life book *This Fabulous Century: 1950–1960,* the editors include a list of the most popular slang phrases used by teenagers on the home front during the Korean War. The following are a few of them and their translations:

Cool: acceptable
Hang loose: don't worry
Wheels: a car
Passion pit: a drive-in movie
Skins: tires
Hairy: scary
Blast-off: go away, get lost
Drag: anyone who becomes a bore

The Nelsons of The Adventures of Ozzie and Harriet *typified the family life many Americans yearned for during the 1950s.*

they offered little more than the image of a perfect married couple with well-adjusted children. The father worked, the mother cooked and cleaned in a home that could pass for any of the numerous Levittown homes, and the children attended school.

The first series, *The Adventures of Ozzie and Harriet,* starred the Nelson family playing themselves. For fourteen seasons and 435 episodes from 1952 to 1966, the parents, Ozzie and Harriet Nelson, along with their two teenage sons, David and Ricky, delighted audiences with their weekly happenings. The topics never included anything more serious than one of the parents forgetting a meeting or one of the boys worrying about the propriety of holding a girl's hand. The family lived in a beautiful two-story home on fictional Sycamore Street, and any tension between the parents and the sons quickly dissolved by show's end. The Nelsons typified the family life that many Americans yearned for.

A second program, still considered one of the classics of television, offered the sole minority member to audiences. *I Love Lucy,* which aired from 1951 to 1961, presented the popular comedienne Lucille Ball and her Cuban American husband, Desi Arnaz. Although the show avoided controversial topics, with the inclusion of Arnaz it at least acknowledged that the United States possessed some ethnic diversity.

The Adventures of Ozzie and Harriet and *I Love Lucy* spawned imitation series that appeared after the war, such as *Leave It to Beaver* and *Father Knows Best,* each dispensing wisdom to children in an effort to impart a moral lesson to the audience. Television critics later assailed these programs for the unrealistic image they conveyed about life in the United States, but at the time they aired, millions of Americans watched precisely because of that image. The complacency and wholesomeness of the portrayed lifestyles offered a counterbalance to the cult of rebellion and national events that shook society.

A Foundation for the Future

The home front during and after the Korean War thus stood as an arena in which

---

Weekly Television Viewing

In the fifties, for the first time in the nation's history, television became an important part of life for the vast majority of people. Television's immense viewing audience hit other forms of entertainment hard—both books and Hollywood films suffered a decline because so many people stayed home and watched television.

In their book *This Fabulous Century: 1950–1960,* the editors at Time-Life printed a typical weekly television schedule for the week of April 4, 1953. The information below comes from that table.

Sunday: *Victory at Sea,* a World War II documentary
See It Now with Edward R. Murrow
Toast of the Town, a variety show hosted by Ed Sullivan and featuring the Notre Dame Glee Club

Monday: *George Burns and Gracie Allen,* a comedy
I Love Lucy, the top-rated show

Tuesday: *The Dinah Shore Show,* a variety show
Featherweight Bout, a boxing match
The Ernie Kovacs Show, a comedy-variety show

Wednesday: *The Perry Como Show,* a variety show
Professional Basketball Playoffs

Thursday: *You Bet Your Life,* a quiz show starring comedian Groucho Marx
Dragnet, a police drama

Friday: *The Adventures of Ozzie and Harriet*
The Life of Riley, a comedy
Our Miss Brooks, a comedy about a teacher

Saturday: *Mr. Wizard,* an educational show about the world of science
Johnny Jupiter, a satire about life on earth as seen by the inhabitants of Jupiter
Your Hit Parade, a musical program presenting that week's best-selling songs

diverse forces grappled with each other—democracy with communism, prosperity with sacrifice, teens with parents, the fiction of family television shows with the reality of society, freedom in concept with the lack of freedom in practice, uniformity with individuality. Citizens of all ages strove to live happy lives, but they faced an unsettled world that, for the first time, possessed the weapons with which it could destroy itself. This resulting tension and insecurity pervaded society and created an existence that stood in stark contrast to the image of the peaceful, comfortable time that many like to recall.

Yet the home front during these years helped lay the foundation for much that was good. The nation was about to enter a prosperous period of its history, partially propelled by consumers willing and able to purchase new products and live in different locations. The infant television industry emerged as a potent source of news and entertainment, in part due to the stunning spectacles of the Kefauver Committee and the demise of Senator Joseph McCarthy. Finally, the roots of the cataclysmic civil rights movement of the 1960s, led by Martin Luther King Jr., took hold on the actions in the country and in the military during the early 1950s.

The home front during the Korean War may not have rivaled its predecessor in World War II, but the impact may have been as important.

★ Notes ★

Introduction: A Different Kind of Home Front

1. Quoted in Douglas T. Miller and Marion Nowak, *The Fifties: The Way We Really Were.* Garden City, NY: Doubleday, 1977, p. 8.
2. Quoted in Miller and Nowak, *The Fifties,* p. 10.

Chapter 1: "Now a Different World"

3. Quoted in David Halberstam, *The Fifties.* New York: Villard Books, 1993, p. 26.
4. Quoted in Halberstam, *The Fifties,* pp. 98–99.
5. Quoted in Miller and Nowak, *The Fifties,* p. 43.
6. Quoted in Paul Boyer, *By the Bomb's Early Light.* New York: Pantheon Books, 1985, p. 350.
7. Quoted in Boyer, *By the Bomb's Early Light,* p. 350.
8. Quoted in Eric F. Goldman, *The Crucial Decade—and After: America, 1945–1960.* New York: Vintage Books, 1960, pp. 136–37.
9. Quoted in Miller and Nowak, *The Fifties,* p. 50.
10. Quoted in Goldman, *The Crucial Decade,* p. 263.
11. Quoted in Spencer C. Tucker, ed., *The Encyclopedia of the Korean War.* New York: Checkmark Books, 2002, p. 161.

Chapter 2: "Embroilment in a Hopeless Cause"

12. Quoted in Goldman, *The Crucial Decade,* p. 159.
13. Quoted in Max Hastings, *The Korean War.* New York: Touchstone, 1987, p. 61.
14. Quoted in Hastings, *The Korean War,* p. 61.
15. Quoted in Hastings, *The Korean War,* p. 81.
16. Quoted in Goldman, *The Crucial Decade,* p. 177.
17. Quoted in Halberstam, *The Fifties,* p. 62.
18. Quoted in Goldman, *The Crucial Decade,* p. 178.
19. Quoted in David McCullough, *Truman.* New York: Simon and Schuster, 1992, p. 813.
20. Quoted in McCullough, *Truman,* pp. 790–91.
21. Quoted in Goldman, *The Crucial Decade,* p. 201.
22. Quoted in Goldman, *The Crucial Decade,* pp. 198–99.

Chapter 3: Conducting an Unpopular War

23. Quoted in Herbert Agar, *The Price of Power: America Since 1945.* Chicago: University of Chicago Press, 1957, p. 129.

24. Quoted in McCullough, *Truman*, p. 838.
25. Quoted in McCullough, *Truman*, p. 845.
26. Quoted in Goldman, *The Crucial Decade*, p. 205.
27. Quoted in Goldman, *The Crucial Decade*, p. 209.
28. Quoted in McCullough, *Truman*, p. 849.
29. Quoted in McCullough, *Truman*, p. 853.
30. Quoted in Spencer C. Tucker, ed., *The Encyclopedia of the Korean War.* New York: Checkmark Books, 2002, p.404.
31. Quoted in Goldman, *The Crucial Decade*, p. 217.
32. Quoted in Hastings, *The Korean War*, p. 317.
33. Quoted in Hastings, *The Korean War*, p. 326.
34. Quoted in Hastings, *The Korean War*, p. 326.
35. Quoted in Goldman, *The Crucial Decade*, p. 248.

Chapter 4: Senator Joseph McCarthy and the Red Scare

36. Quoted in Michael Barson and Steven Heller, *Red Scared! The Commie Menace in Propaganda and Popular Culture.* San Francisco: Chronicle Books, 2001, p. 90.
37. Quoted in Miller and Nowak, *The Fifties*, p. 29
38. Quoted in Miller and Nowak, *The Fifties*, p. 38
39. Quoted in Barson and Heller, *Red Scared!*, p. 111.
40. Quoted in Halberstam, *The Fifties*, p. 50.
41. Quoted in Halberstam, *The Fifties*, p. 55.
42. Quoted in Goldman, *The Crucial Decade*, p. 213.
43. Quoted in Miller and Nowak, *The Fifties*, p. 30.
44. Quoted in McCullough, *Truman*, p. 814.
45. Quoted in Miller and Nowak, *The Fifties*, p. 318.
46. Quoted in Miller and Nowak, *The Fifties*, p. 336.
47. Quoted in Miller and Nowak, *The Fifties*, p. 337.
48. Quoted in Barson and Heller, *Red Scared!*, p. 103.
49. Quoted in Agar, *The Price of Power*, p. 113.
50. Quoted in Agar, *The Price of Power*, pp. 112–13.
51. Quoted in Goldman, *The Crucial Decade*, p. 253.
52. Quoted in Goldman, *The Crucial Decade*, p. 276.
53. Quoted in Goldman, *The Crucial Decade*, p. 276.
54. Quoted in Goldman, *The Crucial Decade*, pp. 277–8.
55. Quoted in Goldman, *The Crucial Decade*, p. 278.

Chapter 5: A Longing for Complacency and Conformity

56. Quoted in Miller and Nowak, *The Fifties*, p. 147.
57. Quoted in Halberstam, *The Fifties*, p. 135.
58. Quoted in Miller and Nowak, *The Fifties*, p. 133.
59. Quoted in Halberstam, *The Fifties*, p. 132.
60. Quoted in Miller and Nowak, *The Fifties*, p. 135.
61. Quoted in Halberstam, *The Fifties*, p. 140.

62. Quoted in Halberstam, *The Fifties*, p. 172.

63. Quoted in Halberstam, *The Fifties*, p. 170.

Chapter 6: Full Democracy at Home

64. Quoted in Arthur Weinberg, ed., *Attorney for the Damned*. New York: Simon and Schuster, 1957, p. 262.

65. Quoted in Miller and Nowak, *The Fifties*, p. 199.

66. Quoted in Halberstam, *The Fifties*, p. 141.

67. Quoted in Miller and Nowak, *The Fifties*, p. 183.

68. Quoted in Tucker, *The Encyclopedia of the Korean War*, p. 11.

69. Quoted in Goldman, *The Crucial Decade*, p. 176.

70. Quoted in Goldman, *The Crucial Decade*, p. 183.

71. Quoted in Goldman, *The Crucial Decade*, p. 185.

72. Quoted in John Hope Franklin, *From Slavery to Freedom*. New York: Alfred A. Knopf, 1974, p. 464.

73. Quoted in Bernard C. Nalty, *Strength for the Fight*. New York: Free, 1986, p. 263.

74. Quoted in Goldman, *The Crucial Decade*, pp. 184–85.

75. Melba Patillo Beals, *Warriors Don't Cry*. New York: Pocket Books, 1994, p. 6.

76. Quoted in Franklin, *From Slavery to Freedom*, p. 421.

77. Quoted in Franklin, *From Slavery to Freedom*, p. 421.

78. Quoted in Franklin, *From Slavery to Freedom*, p. 422.

Chapter 7: Youth Rebellion

79. Quoted in Halberstam, *The Fifties*, p. 482.

80. Quoted in Miller and Nowak, *The Fifties*, p. 280.

81. Quoted in Miller and Nowak, *The Fifties*, pp. 286–87.

82. Quoted in Halberstam, *The Fifties*, p. 481.

83. Quoted in Miller and Nowak, *The Fifties*, p. 287.

84. Quoted in Miller and Nowak, *The Fifties*, p. 302.

85. Quoted in Miller and Nowak, *The Fifties*, p. 305.

86. Quoted in Miller and Nowak, *The Fifties*, p. 291.

87. Quoted in Miller and Nowak, *The Fifties*, p. 302.

88. Quoted in Miller and Nowak, *The Fifties*, p. 304.

89. Quoted in A Tribute to Marlon Brando. http://brando.crosscity.com.

90. Quoted in Goldman, *The Crucial Decade*, p. 119.

91. Quoted in Hastings, *The Korean War*, p. 331.

☆ Chronology ☆

1947

March 12: President Truman issues the Truman Doctrine, committing the nation to the containment of communism.

March 22: President Truman issues Executive Order 9835, calling for loyalty tests for government workers.

June: The United States announces the Marshall Plan, a package of economic and financial aid to Europe.

1948

July 26: President Truman issues Executive Order 9981, calling for the complete integration of the armed forces.

1949

April: The United States joins other democratic nations to form the North Atlantic Treaty Organization (NATO).

September 3: The Soviet Union conducts its first atom bomb test.

1950

January: Alger Hiss is convicted of perjury.

February: Klaus Fuchs is arrested.

February 9: Senator Joseph McCarthy reveals his supposed list of suspected Communists working in the State Department.

May: The U.S. Senate examines the criminal underworld by forming the Special Committee to Investigate Organized Crime in Interstate Commerce.

June 25: Communist forces from North Korea invade South Korea and start the Korean War.

June 27: President Truman announces he is sending American troops to fight in Korea.

July 3: *Time* magazine features William J. Levitt on its cover.

September 15: General Douglas MacArthur launches the surprise attack at Inchon.

November 26: Chinese Communist forces enter the Korean War.

1951

I Love Lucy debuts; *See It Now* debuts; African American Harvey E. Clark faces hostile white reaction to his move into an all-white suburb of Chicago, Illinois; Cleveland disc jockey Alan Freed introduces rock-and-roll music to radio audiences; author Mickey Spillane publishes his novel *One Lonely Night*.

January: President Truman announces wage and price controls; scandals hit both the City College of New York, whose basketball team was involved in illegal betting on games, and West Point, where cadets cheated on examinations; Congress passes the McCarran Internal Security Act, requiring all known Communists to register with the government.

April: President Truman relieves General Douglas MacArthur.

May: Congressional hearings into the Mac-Arthur dismissal begin.

1952

The first issue of *TV Guide* appears; *The Adventures of Ozzie and Harriet* debuts; the U.S. Supreme Court allows public schools to grant release time to students for religious instruction.

March 29: President Truman announces he will not seek reelection in the fall.

April 8: President Truman seizes control of the steel plants.

August: Kemmons Wilson opens his first Holiday Inn.

October 24: Dwight D. Eisenhower states in a Detroit, Michigan, campaign speech that, if elected, he would travel to Korea.

November: The United States conducts its first hydrogen bomb test on November 1; Dwight D. Eisenhower is elected president; Eisenhower travels to Korea.

1953

Sam Phillips discovers Elvis Presley; Ethel and Julius Rosenberg are executed for treason; President Eisenhower issues Executive Order 10450, calling for the investigation of all new government workers; annual sales of the Bible reach 10 million; a settlement ending the fighting in Korea is reached on July 27.

1954

The U.S. Senate opens its investigation of Senator Joseph McCarthy; Congress adds the words "under God" to the Pledge of Allegiance; Ray Kroc expands the McDonald's hamburger chain; the army completes its integration; *Father Knows Best* debuts; Bill Haley's "Shake, Rattle, and Roll" hits the music charts; Marlon Brando stars in *The Wild One*.

March 9: Edward R. Murrow presents his scathing profile of Senator Joseph McCarthy on his program *See It Now*.

May 17: The U.S. Supreme Court issues its famous ruling in the *Brown v. Board of Education* case.

December 2: The U.S. Senate condemns Senator McCarthy, thereby ending his campaign of fear.

1955

Emmett Till is murdered in Mississippi on August 24; James Dean dies in an automobile accident; *Blackboard Jungle* depicts high school juvenile delinquency; the Soviet Union conducts its first hydrogen bomb test on November 22.

1956

Congress unanimously adopts a national motto, "In God We Trust."

1957

Leave It to Beaver debuts; Joseph McCarthy dies of cirrhosis of the liver on May 2.

⋆ For Further Reading ⋆

Books

Charles George, *Life Under the Jim Crow Laws.* San Diego: Lucent Books, 2000. The struggle in the fifties to gain improved conditions for African Americans is vividly portrayed in this valuable book.

Richard Goldstein, *Mine Eyes Have Seen.* New York: Simon and Schuster, 1997. This fascinating collection of first-person accounts helps the reader grasp key currents in the country's history.

Joy Hakim, *All the People.* New York: Oxford University Press, 1995. Part of the author's acclaimed multivolume history of the United States, this book covers many of the events that rocked the fifties.

Phillip Hoose, *We Were There, Too! Young People in U.S. History.* New York: Melanie Kroupa Books, 2001. Hoose has gathered an interesting collection of first-person accounts, representing teenagers who were present at crucial events in American history. Some of the accounts pertain to the fifties.

Stuart A. Kallen, *A Cultural History of the United States Through the Decades: The 1950s.* San Diego: Lucent Books. 1999. The teenage market would find Kallen's volume fun to read as well as informative. The author examines the cultural trends, including television and music, that marked the decade.

Frank B. Latham, *The Rise and Fall of "Jim Crow," 1865–1964.* New York: Franklin Watts, 1969. Latham offers a readable survey of the experience of African Americans in post–Civil War U.S. history. He is helpful in describing the 1950s and 1960s.

William E. Leuchtenburg, *The Great Age of Change.* New York: Time, 1964. Noted historian Leuchtenburg delivers a comprehensive examination of the years 1945 to 1960. The volume would be helpful to anyone looking for a basic understanding of the period.

Linda R. Monk, ed., *Ordinary Americans.* New York: Close Up, 1994. Monk presents numerous eyewitness narratives. Rather than offer the experiences of major figures, she focuses on unheralded people.

Rosa Parks with Jim Haskins, *Rosa Parks: My Story.* New York: Scholastic, 1992. Anyone who wants to understand the civil rights movement that flared during the fifties needs to know about this remarkable woman. Haskins delivers a fine account of her time and struggle.

Flip Schulke and Penelope McPhee, *King Remembered.* New York: Pocket Books, 1986. This biography offers much helpful material pertaining to the start of the 1950s civil rights movement.

Dorothy Sterling, *Tear Down the Walls! A History of the American Civil Rights Movement.* Garden City, NY: Doubleday, 1968. This book is indispensable for understanding the nation's long saga in civil rights. Its chapters covering the 1950s are useful for the reader.

Adam Woog, *The History of Rock and Roll.* San Diego: Lucent Books, 1999. Any reader desiring to understand the roots of rock and roll should consult this book. Written for the junior high student, the book includes numerous photographs and much illuminating information.

Websites

Fifties Web (www.fiftiesweb.com). This site contains all sorts of information about the decade, including movies, popular history, television, and personalities. This fun and educational site is worth exploring.

Levittown: Documents of an Ideal American Suburb (http://tigger.uic.edu). Numerous photographs support the informational text in this lively website of America's first suburbs. Readers will wind up spending more time in this site than planned. The site is hosted by the University of Illinois at Chicago.

National Archives (Britain): Learning Curve (http://learningcurve.pro.gov.uk). Superb material, including illustrations, is presented by this website dealing with the history of the Cold War.

A Tribute to Marlon Brando (http://brando.crosscity.com). This fan website offers a multitude of Brando images and film summaries.

United States of America Korean War Commemoration (http://korea50.army.mil). This government website commemorates the Korean War by offering a multitude of interviews, short biographies, and histories of the conflict. It contains helpful links to other websites.

★ Works Consulted ★

Herbert Agar, *The Price of Power: America Since 1945*. Chicago: University of Chicago Press, 1957. Written shortly after the Korean War, Agar's book accurately conveys the fear that existed in the United States in the early 1950s.

Michael Barson and Steven Heller, *Red Scared! The Commie Menace in Propaganda and Popular Culture*. San Francisco: Chronicle Books, 2001. Adults as well as junior high school students will enjoy this fascinating collection of movies, television programs, and comics that dealt with the issue of communism. Numerous movie posters and television script summaries make this book a treasure.

Melba Patillo Beals, *Warriors Don't Cry*. New York: Pocket Books, 1994. Beals, one of the original nine African American students to integrate Little Rock Central High School in Arkansas, has written one of the most powerful memoirs pertaining to the civil rights struggle of the 1950s. Every teenager should read this book.

Paul Boyer, *By the Bomb's Early Light*. New York: Pantheon Books, 1985. Boyer's original book examines the American response to the growing arms race. He presents numerous examples of American thought, from books, magazines, and film, and shows the fear that gripped the nation in those turbulent years.

Andrew Carroll, ed., *War Letters*. New York: Scribner, 2001. Carroll assembles hundreds of letters from every conflict in American history. He includes those written by famous leaders, the common foot soldier, and their families and friends back home. A wonderful book for revealing the emotions on both the fighting front and the home front.

Editors of Time-Life, *This Fabulous Century: 1950–1960*. New York: Time-Life Books, 1970. This wonderful collection of words, profiles, pictures, and charts makes reading about the fifties fun and exciting.

John Hope Franklin, *From Slavery to Freedom*. New York: Alfred A. Knopf, 1974. This eminent civil rights historian wrote one of the finest surveys of African Americans in U.S. history. He includes some helpful information on events before, during, and after the Korean War.

Eric F. Goldman, *The Crucial Decade—and After: America, 1945–1960*. New York: Vintage Books, 1960. Without a doubt, Goldman has crafted one of the finest accounts of the United States at home during the Korean War. His beautiful writing style captures the drama and intensity of the decade, from the nuclear race to McCarthyism.

David Halberstam, *The Fifties*. New York: Villard Books, 1993. Halberstam offers a superb examination of the decade in this volume. Among other topics, he ably presents material on the Communist scare, the rise of suburbs, and the impact of television on the nation. This is a must for anyone seeking to learn more about the 1950s.

Brett Harvey, *The Fifties: A Women's Oral History*. New York: HarperCollins, 1993. Harvey compiles an intriguing look at the decade from the female point of view. The numerous oral accounts provide a unique glimpse at life in that decade.

Max Hastings, *The Korean War*. New York: Touchstone, 1987. Military historian Max Hastings offers a comprehensive examination of the Korean War. Though he focuses on the military aspects, he also shows the war's effects on the home front.

Alexander Kendrick, *Prime Time*. Boston: Little, Brown, 1969. Kendrick delivers a powerful biography of a fascinating individual whose courage in standing up to Senator Joseph McCarthy marked a high point in journalism. This book contains superb material on Edward R. Murrow's confrontation with the politician.

David McCullough, *Truman*. New York: Simon and Schuster, 1992. David McCullough, the author of several highly regarded biographies and histories, again works his magic with this life of President Harry Truman. McCullough's moving descriptions of Truman's clash with Senator McCarthy and of the president's reactions to criticism over the way he handled the war are particularly powerful.

Douglas T. Miller and Marion Nowak, *The Fifties: The Way We Really Were*. Garden City, NY. Doubleday, 1977. Thoroughly researched and well written, Miller and Nowak's book entertains and educates. This is a superb place to start for anyone interested in the fifties.

Bernard C. Nalty, *Strength for the Fight*. New York: Free, 1986. Nalty's book details the African American struggle for equality in the armed forces. The unique volume contains much interesting information and shows the effects of the Korean War on civil rights.

Colin Shindler, *Hollywood Goes to War*. London: Routledge & Kegan Paul, 1979. Shindler's survey of American films made during World War II and the Korean War is helpful for understanding the general mood of paranoia that swept the nation and was reflected in movies.

I.F. Stone, *The Haunted Fifties*. New York: Merlin, 1963. Stone, a respected news columnist who doggedly battled for individual rights in an era of conformity, suspicion, and rumor, compiled this collection of his columns written during the 1950s. The sharply expressed views give the reader much to think about.

John Toland, *In Mortal Combat: Korea, 1950–1953*. New York: Quill, 1991. Toland brings his lively writing touch to the story of the Korean War. His account will fascinate the reader and help explain the events of the war, particularly those that occurred on the battlefields.

Spencer C. Tucker, ed., *The Encyclopedia of the Korean War.* New York: Checkmark Books, 2002. One of the finest encyclopedias in print, Tucker's book contains readable information on scores of topics concerning the Korean War and the home front.

Arthur Weinberg, ed., *Attorney for the Damned.* New York: Simon and Schuster, 1957. The editor has compiled a collection of the powerful courtroom arguments of Clarence Darrow, one of the most esteemed lawyers in American history. Darrow's words in behalf of African Americans move the reader more than seventy years after uttering them in trial.

Stephen J. Whitfield, *A Death in the Delta.* Baltimore: Johns Hopkins University Press, 1988. Whitfield examines the death of Emmett Till in this book and shows how the murder helped fuel the civil rights movement.

☆ Index ☆

✯ Picture Credits ✯

Cover: © Hulton Archive by Getty Images
AP Wide World, 17, 47
© Bettmann/CORBIS, 12, 52, 59, 71, 75, 83, 91
Courtesy Dwight D. Eisenhower Library, 27
Courtesy Harry S. Truman Library, 44
© Hulton Archive by Getty Images, 15, 21, 23, 25, 34, 49, 55, 61, 62, 65, 72, 76, 78, 79, 97, 99, 100, 103, 106
Library of Congress, 18, 41, 50, 87, 92
The Museum of Modern Art/Film Still Archive, 56
National Archives, 29, 33, 38, 85
© Maj. Earnest A. Staples Jr., USA (Ret.), 89

☆ About the Author ☆

John F. Wukovits is a junior high school teacher and writer from Trenton, Michigan, who specializes in history and biography. Besides biographies of Anne Frank, Jim Carrey, Michael J. Fox, Stephen King, and Martin Luther King Jr. for Lucent Books, he has written biographies of the World War II commander Admiral Clifton Sprague, Barry Sanders, Tim Allen, Jack Nicklaus, Vince Lombardi, and Wyatt Earp. He is also the author of many books about World War II, including the July 2003 book *Pacific Alamo: The Battle for Wake Island*. A graduate of the University of Notre Dame, Wukovits is the father of three daughters—Amy, Julie, and Karen.